Finding Your
JOY

Finding Your
JOY

Real Estate Agent Reflections

GLORIA MARTINDALE

This book is a work of non-fiction. Unless otherwise noted, the author and the publisher make no explicit guarantees as to the accuracy of the information contained in this book and in some cases, names of people and places have been altered to protect their privacy.

Archway Publishing books may be ordered through booksellers or by contacting:

Archway Publishing
1663 Liberty Drive
Bloomington, IN 47403
www.archwaypublishing.com
844-669-3957

Because of the dynamic nature of the Internet, any web addresses or links contained in this book may have changed since publication and may no longer be valid. The views expressed in this work are solely those of the author and do not necessarily reflect the views of the publisher, and the publisher hereby disclaims any responsibility for them.

Any people depicted in stock imagery provided by Getty Images are models, and such images are being used for illustrative purposes only. Certain stock imagery © Getty Images.

Photography by Debra Reyes.

All scriptural references are to the English Standard Version (ESV) of the Bible.

ISBN: 978-1-6657-5869-7 (sc)
ISBN: 978-1-6657-5871-0 (hc)
ISBN: 978-1-6657-5870-3 (e)

Library of Congress Control Number: 2024906768

Print information available on the last page.

Archway Publishing rev. date: 08/07/2024

To my husband, Mark.
My appreciation and love for you are beyond measure.
Thank you for your enduring love, support, and friendship.
You are a perpetual gift.

Additionally, to every person who has provided
wisdom and encouragement in my life. You have made
a real difference, and I appreciate you greatly.

CONTENTS

My Story 1
A Fresh Start 11
Your Story...20
Your Home 25
The Foundation 28
    Connection to God 29
    True Identity 34
    Healing Trauma 37
    Quality People 38
    Proper Alignment 40
Plumbing 42
    Flow of Thoughts...43
    Faith or Fear 46
    Control and Surrender 49
HVAC..52
    Spirit and Soul 52
    True Success..54
Electrical..57
    Desires of Your Heart...57
    Things You Believe 62
    Words Have Power...64
    Daily Activities 65

The Roof 68

  High Standards 68

  Honesty 69

  Serving with Humility 71

The Windows and Screens 74

  Vision and Boundaries 74

  Helping Others 76

  Laughter 78

  Danger in Reviews 79

Cosmetic Finishes 83

  Healthy Lifestyle 83

  Appearance 85

  People Are People 86

Environmental 90

  Eliminate Pests 90

  The People Around You 93

  Your Critics 95

  Relationships 98

Make It Sparkle 101

  Master Your Words 102

  Make Sure They Know 104

  Keep It Simple 105

Decoration 107

  Curate Your Life 108

  Gratitude 110

Hanging String Lights 113

MY STORY

I grew up in a typical middle-class American home. My dad was a deacon in the Catholic Church and sold office supplies for a large company. He was often gone on business trips, and when he was home, he spent many hours at the church, serving in different ways. He would prepare the church for special events and services, and he would preach, counsel people, visit the sick, and bless people's homes. Because he was so busy, it was not easy to find time to spend with him. My best bet was to catch him working in his home office, when he was in town. I would pop into his office when I walked in from school, sit on the recliner, and tell him about my day while he worked.

There is only a handful of times that I remember getting to spend quality time with my dad one-on-one. For instance, there was a rare occasion, when I was about eight years old, that he took me out for pizza, just the two of us. I dressed up in a light pink Cabbage Patch sweater and a hot pink skirt for this rare date with him and I don't remember ever feeling as special as I did when spending that time with him.

My dad jokingly called my mom "Tasmanian devil" because she moved at a tornado-like speed as she rushed around, trying to do way too many things. She stayed home with the kids, took care of the house, and often overcommitted herself to helping others outside our home with all of their projects. Even with all that she had going on, there was always something cooking in our house, and it usually smelled like garlic from the beans, fresh tortillas, or hot grease from the sopaipillas she made for our afternoon snack. Although I had wonderful parents, I experienced some serious stresses throughout my childhood. As an adult, talking to my counselor, I found out that there is a clinical term for what I experienced: complex trauma. Complex trauma describes a child's exposure to multiple traumatic events, often of an invasive, interpersonal nature, and the wide-ranging, long-term effects of this exposure.

When I was seven months old, my nine-year-old brother was crossing the street to play baseball with his friends and was hit by a drunk driver. He was dragged under the truck for about a block. When my mom ran into the house covered in blood, my two older sisters found out that their brother was dead. I was a baby and crying on the lap of one of my sisters who, until that day, had never held me. She was scared of holding a baby, but that day she had no choice.

From this time onward, my family was heavy with grief for many years. In fact, shortly after my brother's death, my mom took me to the doctor to find out what was wrong with me because after he died, I literally did not cry or make a sound for months. They even forgot me at home one day because I was so quiet. The doctor said that I was depressed. That was the only explanation he could give her. Every person in our family was struggling in different ways as they processed their individual grief. My older sisters said that our family used to go camping and do fun things as a family, but this stopped after my brother died.

Our family did not engage in counseling or even talk much about our feelings. This is just not something that we did. My dad would joke that counseling was "foofoo" and "voodoo quackery," yet he counseled people at church all the time. Part of me believes that he did not want to face his own issues at this time as I know he had some heavy things to unpack from his youth. I think he was more comfortable keeping it all tightly packed in for fear that if anything loosened, things would be much worse. I don't think there is a perfect way to handle stress and trauma, but I do know that by not handling it, the problems in my family were magnified. To compound this, there were constantly other struggles in our home as time went on. My dad had familial polyposis, a hereditary disease. Polyps, little round growths, were continually accumulating in his intestines. He regularly had to get sections of his intestines removed because the polyps become cancerous. My two older sisters inherited this disease and were already dealing with surgeries when they were around ten and twelve years old. There were several times throughout childhood when I was worried about my dad dying, especially one time when he had to be flown to Cleveland for specialized surgery that only one doctor in the US could do. I also remember visiting one of my sisters in the hospital, and she looked so horrible that I thought it was the last time I would see her alive.

My younger sister's struggle with serious mental illness was another factor. This began when we were young children. When I was eight years old and she was four, she had an adorable Afro of curly hair, and she would literally stand in front of the mirror, scream, and use both fists to rip her hair out of her head. This was our first indication that there was something wrong. My mom was overwhelmed by issues like this, and no one could ever diagnose what was going on with her until she had a true mental breakdown right before her high school finals. This was when we found out that she had schizoaffective disorder, a combined diagnosis of schizophrenia and bipolar disorder. She would experience extreme emotions, delusions, disorganized speech, and trouble thinking clearly, and she struggled to interact with others in society.

Our family had many issues, and my parents had their hands

full. My mom was grieving and stressed while caring for four daughters, especially with my dad traveling often for work. My younger sister needed a lot of attention, and my mom relied on me to do whatever it took to keep her quiet, so that's what I did. I played her games and spent much of my time as a child attending to her.

Beyond all of this, there were family members engaged in drug abuse and alcoholism, experiences with abuse by family members and neighbors, and my mom's struggle with breast cancer as I entered high school. I was constantly worried about my mom for years and wondering when my time with her would come to an end. Dressed up for my senior prom, I took my date to the hospital so that my mom could see us before we went out. At that time, she had lost all of her hair from chemo and was going through bone marrow transfusions. The sadness I felt, plus the sadness of every-one around me relating to her illness, was a pretty heavy feeling to carry around. It was awful to see her struggle. It was like looking over the edge of a cliff, waiting to be pushed off.

Looking back on all of the experiences in my upbringing, I often felt alone and unseen, and I felt an unreasonable amount of responsibility to deal with everything, mostly without the help or support of others. However, I don't think anyone in my family knew how to process what they were individually going through or what we were collectively going through, so we just kept going.

In addition to all that was happening around me that I could not control, I created some terrible experiences on my own, in both small and big ways. High school was an intensely crazy time for me, but at the time, it seemed normal. I had gotten introduced to drinking at an early age by one of my older family members, who poured a punch bowl full of jungle juice made with Everclear for my eighth-grade friends and gave us straws to drink up and enjoy the "fun." That same year, my best friend's mom was a single mom and a stripper who typically worked all weekend. When I stayed the night at her house, we would end up at strange parties, and one night we decided that we should take her mom's car to the movies. Of course, at that age, my friend did not have a driver's license, and as we drove, my friend gave me a hit of acid—and she took one as well. I can't even imagine how we are still alive.

Another night, the summer before tenth grade, after my dad transferred me to a private Catholic school in hopes of connecting me with better influences, I went to a party that was thrown by men in their twenties. I was taken there by my "big buddies" who had been introduced to me through the private school. While I was there, one of my new friends ran out of a room crying, and I found out that she had been raped by one of these men. My group of friends rushed to leave, but one of the men pressed a gun against the side of my head and told me I could not leave. Luckily I was not shot when I shoved my arm against his, pushed the gun away from my head, and ran to the car.

As I got into high school, I was binge drinking and smoking marijuana on a regular basis with friends. Driving from a party under the influence of drugs and alcohol as I was headed to my midnight-shift job, I totaled my first car and felt relief that one of my best friends at the time, who was in the passenger seat, was unharmed. The steel pole from the fence we ran into literally crushed the front of my car like an accordion and stopped at the windshield right between the two of us.

The summer after graduating high school, I got involved with an older man. As a special treat, he took me out of the country to have lunch in Mexico. I was so excited to be getting this atten-tion, and to be doing something so out of the ordinary, that I was blinded to what was really happening. Apparently he and a friend had a plan to load the car up with drugs while we were eating lunch. When we had finished lunch, I unknowingly rode back in the car that his friend had loaded with drugs. He drove them to the US border with me in the car! To my shock he was arrested at the border, and I had to make the dreaded phone call to my dad to tell him what had happened and ask him to come and get me. Can you imagine what it felt like to make this call? I quickly broke up with the boyfriend, and when he was released from jail, I was stalked by him for a period of time. I would notice cars following me or receive messages from him through my boss at work after I had blocked communication from him. I also received threats from his dad, who told me he would break my dad's legs if I did not do the things they wanted me to do. Thankfully, my dad would not allow me to live in fear and dismissed the threats. Of course this was extremely disruptive and unsettling. Clearly I was not making good decisions, and my life was chaotic.

Through it all, I always kept my grades up and was an excellent student from elementary school through college. It's like I was living the lives of two different people. One was respectful during the day at school, getting excellent grades, doing community service, and the things I was supposed to do; I was going to church regularly and was trying to be a good person. On the other hand, I was sneaking out of the house, doing things I shouldn't do, and getting into trouble outside school. I did not have clarity about what I wanted in life, and my self-esteem was low so I allowed others to choose for me. When I was at school, my parents and teachers told me to excel, and I did. When I was not at school, many of the friends who surrounded me influenced me to do things that were negative and destructive to my life and my future. I went along with a lot of things I shouldn't have.

Fast-forward to my early twenties. People looking at my life from the outside might have thought I had it all. I was finishing up my degree at UNM on a full-ride scholarship at Anderson School of Business, one of the country's top business schools. I met my now ex-husband in an astronomy class and we became study partners. Later we owned a successful real estate and mortgage brokerage, and there was a big banner with my name and picture on it hanging on a building in downtown Albuquerque, where I would be the driving force for selling the very first loft development that the city had ever seen.

I was a regular at spin and yoga classes and took good care of my body and my image. I bought expensive clothing and drove BMWs, Mercedes, and Audis. We had a beautiful custom home that I designed, tucked into the lush landscape of the north valley, with huge cottonwood trees all around. It was a quick walk to the river, where I would run, bike, and breathe in the fresh air. I went to champagne brunch every Friday, and then went to a flower shop to select fresh flower stems for my home. We regularly had friends over to enjoy food, music, and plenty of cocktails that we provided from our floor-to-ceiling stocked liquor cabinet.

My (now ex) husband and I vacationed often, both domestically and internationally, and we were surrounded by friends and luxury. We danced with celebrities at parties and hosted parties for hundreds of friends and clients in a hotel ballroom each year. We would frequent fine-dining restaurants and treat large groups of friends to extravagant meals and drinks.

We had some incredible experiences with a friend who was an NBA player and his wife (who is still my dear friend today). We stood in their wedding party and experienced Brian McKnight's heavenly velvet voice as he played the piano and sang when they walked down the aisle. Then at the wedding reception, he came over to me, took my hand, and led me out to the dance floor—me and Brian McKnight slow dancing! That was one of my favorite experiences during that time.

There are also some other experiences that stand out in my memories of this time. At Kenyon Martin's birthday party, surrounded by captivating people and loud party music, I danced with Allen Iverson. And one New Year's Eve, we sat in a VIP suite at an NBA game, drinking cases of chilled Cristal, and then rode around in a limo, barhopping with NBA players. It felt surreal to have celebrity athletes wearing Rolex watches and fur coats sitting next to me and around me in such close quarters as we traveled together. After all, I was just a normal girl from the northwest suburbs of Albuquerque.

In all that I experienced during this time of abundance, there was still a desert in my spirit. I would not trade those experiences for anything—not because of the shiny, ideal life that I had but because those experiences showed me that *something was missing.* At this time, I regularly felt like an imposter in my own life. I was laughing on the outside but crumbling on the inside.

There were some things I truly loved about my life, like guiding people through real estate transactions and staging homes, spending time in nature, working on art projects, listening to live music, enjoying brunches one-on-one with close friends, and spending time with family. However, in most areas of my life, I was focused on superficial pleasures and was constantly struggling against feelings of unworthiness and melancholy. Part of this was because of unresolved issues from my past, and part of it was because of the choices I had made while building my current life. Due to pressure from a Hispanic culture, and my lack of self-esteem, I had gotten married at twenty-two years old, knowing that my values and my (ex) husband's values were not in alignment. The biblical wisdom about being unequally yoked is real!

In the beginning of the relationship, I was in tears every Sunday as I drove to church by myself, and I eventually stopped going. I worked out all the time, striving to have a perfect body, and even though I was in great shape, I never felt good enough. When we had parties, I was usually filled with anxiety and then would make the subconscious decision to get wasted drunk. I did this to escape the discomfort of all the things in my life that did not represent who I truly was and to fill the void that I felt due to lack of true connection with the people in my life. People would tell me that they "loved drunk Gloria," and this made me feel awful. They didn't mean any harm in saying this, but hearing it made me wonder if people could love the "real Gloria"—or if they even knew her. It also made me feel shame about how much I drank in social settings. I did not have control over my life, and drinking was a simple, easy, and socially acceptable way to cope and to escape.

After the real estate and stock market crash in 2008, I eventually lost my real estate and mortgage business. We also had to give an apartment building back to the bank after completely remodeling it. This apartment building seemed like it would be a quick, uncomplicated fix and flip, but we ran into unexpected challenges that made it impossible to complete. We also got pinned with an $80,000 debt from an investor we had worked with on another property, when he decided to renege on his promise to cover his portion. I had tied my identity to being a successful business owner, and when these projects failed and the market crashed, so did I. I spent endless days alone, crying in bed, and most of the friends who had surrounded me before, including my ex-husband, seemed to vanish as quickly as our lavish lifestyle. No more glamorous parties or extravagant travel. We were forced to sell our custom home and move into a rental. We had built our lifestyle from real estate income, so we found another house, bought it using creative financing help from a family friend, and fixed it up. The house was beautiful once it was completed, and my ex-husband decided to go back to school and start a new career. This was not easy at the time as the market was slow, so I created a line of jewelry that I sold in a couple of boutiques to make it all work.

And after all of this, our marriage suddenly ended in divorce. I was thirty-three years old, and it was difficult to make simple decisions on my own because I lacked self-esteem, confidence, and understanding of who I was. When we separated and I had my own place to live for the first time in my life, it was time to learn more about who I was. I regularly went to counseling and was challenged to do one thing each day for *myself*. Until this time, I had lived trying to please the people around me and being blown from one thing to the next at the whims of others. It was time to start choosing the things I wanted in my life and stop bending to the will of other people. This was something that was extremely challenging for me to change, after a lifetime of being a rudderless ship! I began learning to identify the things I wanted in my life, and even to move past the resistance I received from others, to get what I wanted. I started going to morning mass with my mom every day that I could. As I cried through each service, she would hold my hand and pass me tissues. "Here you go, honey." Her simple gesture of handing me tissues made me feel seen and loved. It felt so healing to be back at church on a regular basis and to spend time with my mom—who was becoming visibly smaller and smaller before my eyes as she continued her twenty-year battle with cancer.

A FRESH START

One year after my divorce, my mom, the person I loved more than anyone in the world, lost her battle with cancer and passed away. My ex-sister-in-law, someone I admired greatly, had invited me several times over the years to attend an ACTS (Adoration, Community, Theology, Service) retreat and asked me again after my mom passed away. She told me that this retreat would change my life in the best possible way, and she seemed to carry a peace and joy that I did not have. I had repeatedly declined the invitation because I was too busy and because I did not believe it would be impactful for me. Deep down, I don't think I believed that something so wonderful could happen for me. With my life now being stripped of busy-ness, and having nothing to lose, I decided to attend an ACTS Retreat.

This retreat was very different from anything I had ever experienced, and this is where the Holy Spirit ignited my life. From this time forward, things were never the same—this time for the better. I came home with a completely different outlook on life, and I became a retreat director after the experience. It was like a huge weight had been lifted from me, and I felt happy and unburdened. My family all commented on the change in me—some with joy for who I was becoming and others with agitation that I was "not the same." The guy I was dating at the time became nervous when I didn't want to drink as much. His dad warned him about "religious" people like me so he broke up with me. I was actually glad. I wanted to be my authentic self and be loved for who I actually was, so I considered this a step in the right direction.

It's really easy to keep friends and loved ones in your corner when you don't grow. Familiar people are oftentimes a "safe harbor" of the life we know. The saying by John A Shedd, "A ship in the harbor is safe, but that is not what ships are built for," is a great way to think of this. When you are growing into more of who you are meant to be, sometimes those relationships no longer work, and that's OK. I loved the new friendships I had formed with the ACTS ladies and the meaningful work of creating the retreat experience for others. However, I knew my time in Albuquerque had come to an end. The real estate market was not recovering in New Mexico, and because I was struggling to find meaningful work, I started searching in Colorado. I would spend hours in the chapel praying about moving. It was such a scary concept because I had never left my family, and in a Hispanic family like mine, it was a very big deal to move away from my tight-knit family. I knew that if I left, the dynamics in my family would never be the same. I did not want to hurt them, but I needed a fresh start.

One year after my mom passed away, I moved to Colorado and started a new life. This was a really big deal for me because I typically struggled to make simple decisions. Imagine how scary that was. Imagine not being sure of most decisions that you had made in the past and deciding to move somewhere where you had to rely only on yourself, and only on your own decisions. With my newfound clarity and confidence in God, I was able to persist against a great deal of resistance in doing something I believed in. Not only did I receive resistance from some of my family, but my financial situation would have stopped most people in their tracks. At that time, I had a little-used Kia Soul that I had not yet paid off, some personal items, and *nothing* in my bank account. Luckily, the morning before I left, I visited my aunt to say goodbye. She handed me a $500 check as a thank-you for the time I had recently spent staging her home for sale. She had no idea how much I needed this money. This was literally all I had as I left for Colorado.

At the time, I was dating someone in Colorado. I wanted just to rent an apartment in his complex to get to know him better, but he insisted that I move in with him. Although I was making huge progress in making my own decisions, I had a weak moment and chose to move in with him. But when I walked into the apartment, I immediately knew it was the wrong decision. I tried to make it work, but it quickly became clearer and clearer that I was not in a good situation, both in the relationship and with living together. One morning when he got angry and abruptly left, I rushed to load my Kia Soul with as many of my personal belongings as I could, packed everything else I owned into boxes, and stacked them in his dining room. I then called an acquaintance in the area to ask if I could live with her family since the apartment I found would not be ready for a month. There were other apartments available, but I wanted to be in a gated community as I felt fearful of being single and alone. I had no other place to go, and I am forever thankful for the kindness they extended to me, allowing me to move in with them. I knew that my belongings might not be there for me when I was ready to pick them up, but I needed to correct the mistake I'd made and was willing to cut my losses. No material possessions were worth living with the results of a bad decision. I didn't have much, but by this time, I had learned that it was better to give up the little I had than to continue down another path that was incongruent with who I was and who I wanted to become. I knew that if I did not act on my convictions, I would just slide back into the same pattern of allowing things to happen to me. Admitting that I had made a big mistake made things more complicated in the short run, but I was proud of myself for getting back on the right course, even though it was not a graceful or pretty sight to behold.

I started my new job at a national homebuilder, knowing that I would have to use credit card advances to secure my apartment and that it would take a while to get ahead. The way I chose to move may have been messy and may have looked like a disaster, but my messiness did not bother God. He did not just watch me fall. Instead He dusted me off and continued to help me as I moved forward.

Upon moving into my apartment and having a beautiful space to myself where I could take a breath after everything I'd been through to get there, I experienced a depth of loneliness like never before. I cried the most gut-wrenching tears as I grieved for my mom and missed my home, my family, friends, ACTS sisters, and all that I knew. I also had the most wonderful feeling of hope for what my future held. I knew I was in between my difficult past and the future I hoped for. There was no way that I was going to turn back, even though I regularly received calls from family members telling me that I just needed to come home. I was now committed to my future.

The colorful natural beauty and fresh air of Colorado brought me joy! I spent time training for half marathons and started biking to work—not to gain that perfect physique that I had once striven for but because I enjoyed it. I enjoyed my job with the homebuilder and the people I worked with. I revamped the entire communication system for the office and created a new system for my own position that allowed me efficiently to manage twice the volume that was being done before, while taking weekends off. I pushed through the initial fear and discomfort of sending daily emails of encouragement to the whole office, and I received gratitude from various coworkers daily for sharing these messages. I was involved in groups at different churches, started building connections, and shared my faith with the people around me. I prayed constantly and depended on God for *everything*.

As I outgrew this position, I prayed that God would open up the right career path—and He did. I went from working for the builder to doubling my pay after getting my Colorado real estate license, selling for a big brokerage where I was recognized as one of the top closers in the country. After a year, I was promoted to managing and coaching a large team of agents, again increasing my annual pay, and being recognized with awards for excellence as a coach. I gained a new kind of confidence, no longer focused on superficial success, and where I embraced the business as my identity—this time on a solid foundation with my eyes on God and the things that matter, things of substance.

My identity is no longer anchored to my superficial success but to who I am in Christ and how I serve Him and the people around me. I am not just confident in my abilities that are tied to my profession, but I believe I am worthy of enjoying all of the benefits in life that God has given me because I am His. This identity is what truly gives life meaning.

While I was working for the homebuilder, I was also praying for the specific qualities I wanted in my future husband. I dated some good guys who were not right for me, and some not-so-great guys in general, but this time I was not going to settle. I knew God wanted more for me. As my online dating subscription drew near the end, I realized that I was really happy on my own. If I didn't find the right person, I was OK with it. I had gotten used to doing things in my own way, making every decision on my own. I had my own routine that I loved, and I would even enjoy going out to eat by myself. This was very different from my unsettled past, where I was continually trying to fill a void or meet someone else's expectations. And to my surprise, the very last date I went on was the answer to my prayer.

Mark is the man who kept me laughing, and in awe of his heart and character, as we texted back and forth for days before we met. When I stood in front of him the first time we met in person, he left me literally speechless because of *who* he was, how attracted I was to him, his deep voice, the warmth of his personality, and the amazement that a person could have this kind of effect on me. He is my soulmate. God was paying attention to my prayers, and despite all of my mistakes and shortcomings, He did not let me down. In addition, I had not let myself down this time by settling for the wrong person. On our second date, we went to a vibrant Christian church together that we had both attended before, where we loved the music and the message each week. From our second date until this day, we have continued practicing our faith together.

In May 2017, after gaining my dad's blessing, we became engaged, planning our wedding for January 2018. In October 2017, my dad found out that his health condition had worsened and he would need very dangerous surgery. In December 2017, a week after making it through the surgery, while still in the hospital, he got an infection in the wound. Because he was not able to make his own decision, a family meeting was called to decide whether to operate again, or to start comfort measures. On December 15, he passed away. As difficult as it was, with grief, and also resistance from some family members, we kept our wedding plans. I knew God had brought us together, and although there was nothing that could take away the sadness and loss that I felt, I knew God had good plans for us—and we chose to treat them with importance and to claim them! I was no longer letting things happen to me like I did from childhood into early adulthood or allowing others to dictate the direction of my life. I continued taking responsibility in choosing the direction that my life would go.

Choosing my own path and destiny when I moved to Colorado and moving forward with my marriage during a difficult time for my family were two very big decisions, and I proved to myself that I had changed in a big way. I let myself out of the prison I was in and empowered myself to *live my life*. My life before was kind of like a quilt where each person around me contributed their thoughts and opinions about how I should live. I was accepting all the scraps they gave me and stitching them into a very distorted-looking quilt. Of course they meant well, but this was creating a dysfunctional life for me. Now one choice at a time, I was creating my own life with a pattern that made much more sense and was pleasing to me. I was living with integrity, and I found that this was a much more beautiful way to live.

After only two years of marriage, and right before the COVID pandemic started, my younger sister, who struggles with a severe case of schizoaffective disorder, moved into our home. Caring for someone with mental illness can take anyone to their limits, and this was an extremely challenging time. Together, we put our trust in God, and again, He did not let us down. We had her in our home for three years, and we allowed God to guide us every step of the way, starting with the decision to care for her. It was incredible how He showed us what to do in every situation and provided all of the support that we needed along the way. This was a time of extreme difficulty but a blessing in so many ways! During this time, we developed new friendships and business connections, and we learned so much more about mental health in general. Laughter filled our house, and I regularly laughed so hard that my stomach hurt. Beyond all of this, it has been clear to see that our marriage is truly built on God's foundation. We worked as a team throughout this time, and because of the way my husband led our family through these difficult times, I have been even more in awe of his wisdom, love, endurance, and substance.

We have a great lifestyle, but it feels much different from the lifestyle I'd had before. We live on a huge farm where we marvel at God's goodness as we experience His creation through incredible sunsets, rows of purple lavender, all of the produce springing to life from tiny seeds and filling up trailers with piles of colorful pumpkins.

I am still involved in real estate, and I'm venturing into other projects that I feel inspired to do. We have two adorable standard poodles, a beautiful and comfortable home, and meaningful work. The abundance we have is deeper than material things, glamor, and fleeting pleasure. It runs deep with the riches of love, respect, clarity, steadiness, joy, forgiveness, acceptance, grace, generosity, vision, gratitude, honor, character, and so much more. I've often felt alone in my life. I now feel deeply connected.

We gain satisfaction from the time we spend purposefully working every day, and we enjoy time together every morning and evening. In the morning, we pray and read the Bible together over coffee and enjoy deep conversation. In the evening, we cook and enjoy dinner together. My husband is an amazing cook, and he regularly takes the time to prepare meals that are special, attending to details and using fresh food and herbs that he grows himself. I usually prepare the side dishes. If he is busy, I sometimes chop up ingredients and then ask him to turn it into something! Then we enjoy our dinner and spend some time together as we unwind from the day. My husband's motto is that we need to "create a life that we don't need a vacation from." We have certainly done this, and we don't travel often. When we do travel, we are present and enjoying each moment. If we are at the beach, we might get lost walking along the beach, revel in the sound of the waves, look for seashells, search for the best gelato or street tacos, or seize the opportunity to swim with dolphins. Sometimes we may not even leave our hotel room, just enjoying each other's company and laughing for hours.

Over the years, we have studied the Bible and prayed together every morning, growing in our understanding of God's word and building a true foundation for life. Our life has been built on love for God, love for each other and the people around us, and challenging each other to grow into the best possible version of ourselves. I've learned that God's riches run deep, and He always has more for us. All we have to do is stay connected to Him, be open to do the work, and receive the blessings He provides.

Think of how it feels to eat a bunch of delicious food that you know is not good for you. Maybe you have a plate of fried foods or some other kind of junk food, some soda, and a dessert. It may taste good, but it doesn't make you feel satisfied and you don't feel very good once the meal is over. There are times you can get everything you think you want, and it does not give you what you *truly* want and need. This is how I felt before I really engaged in a relationship with God and cleaned up my life. Now think about having an incredible meal in a romantic setting where you get your favorite meal. For me, this is a nice, chilled, crispy salad, a perfectly cooked steak and baked potato, and a glass of my favorite wine. After a meal like this, you feel satisfied, and you enjoy the experience. That is how I feel with God in my life and doing the work to create a life that is worth living.

It's a beautiful thing when we wait on God's direction and trust in His ways for every area of our lives. Things may not happen in the way we think they will, but God's guidance simultaneously brings us adventure and peace when we put our trust in Him. I have found that even though I am not perfect and continuously make mistakes, God patiently and lovingly works all things for good and continues to straighten my path as I focus on Him and try to get it right.

The world we live in can be chaotic and sometimes scary. However, no matter what is going on around us, we can remain calm. When we are connected to God, we are standing on His solid foundation of love. God is bigger than any storm that may be raging, and when our focus is on Him, He simply stretches out his arm and the chaos subsides. In the physical world, things seem unstable and chaotic, but spiritually things are already settled. If we tap into all that God has for us, we are not distracted by the raging storm that is threatening to harm us. We are settled in His truth that we are loved and protected. We know that all will work together for good. Our life is fleeting, but He is eternal.

YOUR STORY

Your story may not look the same as mine. However, I believe that no matter what your story is, you can use the same helpful wisdom that I have used in my life to find joy in yours. If you are tired of experiencing the storms of life, personally and in your business, with feelings of instability, turmoil, discomfort, pain, frustration, and lack of clarity, you can do something about it. Finding joy is a process, and it takes commitment. Many people do not experience joy because they have not slowed down and taken the time and effort that are needed to go through the process. This process involves identifying what you want in life, facing the reality of what currently exists, thinking about your options, and choosing what you will do to claim your joy. It takes intention, work, time, and commitment. Whether you stay in your current state or work to change it, it is difficult. You truly have nothing to lose and everything to gain by choosing joy.

My mom used to say that cleanliness is next to godliness. We all long for heaven—the place where we will have perfect purity in our spirit and our environment, fruitfulness, joy, no stress or dysfunction in relationships, and true connection with those around us and our world. No evil, only good! No failure, only success! No hate, only love! No loneliness, only connection! No death, only life! While we won't experience this freedom fully until heaven, we can try to create a life that resembles heaven on earth. In order to accomplish this, we must be willing to look at the areas that need attention. This can be mildly—or extremely—uncomfortable but is well worth it to maximize our lives and help us live in a way that uses the full potential and gifts that God gave us.

You may be thinking that this does not sound like something that will help you sell real estate. I assure you that as you read, absorb, and carry out the lessons, you will find this is exactly what you need to sell real estate—or to do anything else you set your mind on doing. Having integrity is the state of being whole and undivided. When we work to improve any part of who we are, we work toward a greater degree of integrity, which makes us more effective in every area of our lives. Some may believe that they can hide their personal struggles with a veil of professionalism and clever vocabulary. However, contrary to what we may believe, we cannot hide any undesirable qualities we may have, or things we are struggling with, while working with our clients. This is because we are always the same person carrying the same values, beliefs, desires, strengths, and shortcomings into every area of our lives and every activity we perform. Those things that we are trying to hide or suppress will, at some point, make themselves known. Whether it is blatantly obvious or just discreetly noticed by others, it will be revealed. The more we can be in a state of wholeness and willing to bring our whole self into any situation, the better we can be as a spouse, a parent, a friend, and a guide for our clients. When we are operating out of integrity, we are genuine in our dealings, and because of this, we are more productive, have more success, and our lives are more fulfilling and satisfying. Being in this state requires consistent attention and maintenance.

When we do not attend to ourselves and work toward wholeness, this neglect will manifest in heartache, frustration, and lack of fruitfulness. As an illustration, let's think about how this relates to a home. Neglect in a home looks like clutter, uncleanliness, and disrepair. Think about how refreshing it is when you put the attention and work into your home and your surroundings after a period of neglect. Imagine the wonderful feeling of walking in the front door of your home and realizing that all of the junk that was thrown everywhere, all of the dishes that were piled up in the sink, and the film of dust that covered everything are gone. The dishes are sanitized and sparkling, stacked neatly in the cabinets. Every coat is hung where it belongs; there is no clutter, mess, or trash in sight. Even the trash cans have been emptied, cleaned, and sanitized. Every item sparkles, and the windows are so clean that the beautiful view welcomes you home. The smell of your home is fresh, and your favorite scent fills the air. The look of your home is clean, comfortable, and inviting. You are organized and know where everything is, and the decor represents the best version of yourself. The people in your home are happy and peaceful, deeply connected to you. Suddenly, as you look around, taking in your improved environment with all of your senses, you feel over-whelmed with pure happiness, positive energy, love, and peace!

The reality is that life can be busy and complicated, and we may not maintain our home in this way or clean it to this degree. Chances are that most people have unfinished laundry, a pile of dirty dishes, random socks on the floor, cabinets sticky from little fingers, dusty furniture, piles of papers, and closets full of junk. Beyond this, there may even be a foundation issue, a pest infestation, things in disrepair, a foul odor, or other issues that are part of our normal life experienced at home. And beyond our physical environment, most people have trouble with relationships and boundaries, confusion about their goals and purpose, and struggles with money and gaining fulfillment from their work.

Just like the experience of walking through your house after you've attended to every detail in cleaning it up, wouldn't it feel great to turn your attention to any and all areas of your life where there is a need and have that same experience of overall relief? When you have done the work, your relationships are simple and uncomplicated, you have clarity about your life and your purpose, and your business is fruitful. There will always be challenges, but when they appear, you can clearly and easily identify and deal with them because you are not bogged down in other unresolved issues.

When exploring areas that need work, it's important to keep in mind that each of us was wonderfully made, knit together in our mother's womb by our infinitely loving Creator. He does not make mistakes, and He knew what He was doing when He made every part of you, including your mind, quirks, sense of humor, talents, dreams, desires, and all that makes you who you are. There is nothing inherently wrong with you. However, we all have different experiences in life that lead to our struggles. These could be thought patterns we've developed, abusive relationships, stresses we've experienced, differences in upbringing and education, traumatic experiences, disappointments, and more.

Everyone has things they can work on to improve. The more we are willing to look at any unpleasant qualities we may have, or things we need to work on, the more we are able to grow. It's kind of like pruning a beautiful plant that we want to keep healthy. As we cut off the dead matter, new life sprouts! As you read through the opportunities for improvement in the coming pages, remember to be intentional and to lean on God to show you where to focus your attention. There is so much opportunity that it could feel overwhelming. But instead, let the opportunities encourage you because you have infinite potential! We all have it, and it's our choice to ignore it or to claim it.

If you are reading this book on your own, you should spend time writing in a journal to consider the questions in each section and flesh out your thoughts and insights. It may also be helpful to read this book as part of a Bible study or book club with friends. You can use the questions in each section as journal topics or conversation starters to deepen your understanding. Exploring the book in this way will bring it to life and bring about growth and lasting change in your life and in your business.

I will suggest some ways to revitalize your life, using the metaphor of a home being inspected, repaired, and cleaned. Keep in mind that the suggestions are in no particular order and will by no means identify every potential need. Asking God to show you what your focus should be is critical, and you can do this as you read.

I pray that God will bless you with powerful new wisdom and insight as you read this book and that you will have the focus and strength to implement the things you learn. May God calm your storm and bring peace and joy to your life.

YOUR HOME

I use the symbolism of a home inspection because a home is a very sacred place and represents who we are. It should be a place that keeps us safe and sheltered, helps us share life with the people we love the most, and should be the sanctuary we run to after a hard day. If we have really poured out our attention and love into our space, it will be organized and functional and have beautiful decor. Because it is such a personal space, and a space that we have control over to a great degree, I will use this as a symbol of your life, both personal and professional.

Your home may be incredibly beautiful, spacious, and inviting, in a wonderful neighborhood, with charm and striking architectural features, overlooking a gorgeous view. Yet even with all of the desirable qualities of your home, there may be underlying issues. Sometimes, just by being intentional about finding the root of any issues, you can identify them on your own. Other times it's hard to identify what is going on in a home, and you may need to call on experts to uncover any deferred maintenance or defects. A professional and thorough home inspector would discover many underlying concerns in any house. Because we get used to our way of living in our home, it may come as an overwhelming surprise after inspection to find the laundry list of things that are not functioning properly!

Similarly, we as people and real estate agents may want to do some introspection once in a while when we feel a bit off. Maybe life is great overall, but we sense that there are some issues because we continuously run into the same roadblocks, emotional challenges, or setbacks. We may need to enlist the help of a pastor, counselor, spouse, trusted friend, coworker, coach, psychiatrist, or doctor to help us look for clues about what is causing the frustrations, using their knowledge of us and the experience in their particular field. Capturing everything, even the most minor issues, can be overwhelming. Some issues may be easy to resolve, while others may take years or decades to uncover fully. Often issues will surface one at a time, and as you resolve one, another may show up. It's a process that takes patience and the right mindset. If you are in the mindset of *expectancy* that you will identify places within yourself that need healing, *faith* that you can work through each issue you find, and *gratitude* as you overcome each issue, you can grow into all that you were *meant to be.*

With the guidance of the Holy Spirit, we can determine how to move forward, maximizing our potential for a fruitful life. It is so important to remain prayerful and to take God's guidance no matter how foreign it may seem, using discernment to identify what is from God and should be embraced (life-giving, loving thoughts) and what is not and should be dismissed (destructive, condemning thoughts). It is also important to remain open to the way God wants to reveal things, the timing in which He reveals them, and how He wants you to work toward solutions. His way is *always* the best way, so take all that you read here, and any wisdom you get from other places, with an open mind. Allow God to customize the process in a way that only He knows is best for *you.*

- What is clearly going well in your personal life and in your real estate business?
- Do you sense that there are areas with obvious or hidden potential that you should look into more deeply? Why?

- What do you hope to gain from this process?
- Do you believe that you can work through anything that comes to light?
    - Who can you turn to for support?
- How can you celebrate each victory?

Our development process is like a kaleidoscope. Just like a kaleidoscope holds shapes and colors that rotate and shift, we experience a variety of challenges in life. And just like each work of art produced by a kaleidoscope, each and every challenge is made of the same things. The solutions are also made of the same things. It may seem or look different from the time before, but that's an illusion. The truth is that as we turn the dial on the kaleidoscope of life and overcome one challenge, a new challenge is revealed that gives us the opportunity to learn the same lesson on a deeper level, or in a different way. Another way to look at life's challenges and lessons is to think of them like gemstones with many facets. As we examine each facet, we are seeing something different. However, the bigger picture is that we are examining the same stone over and over from different perspectives. Life is all about perspective, and the wisdom we gain in overcoming one challenge is transferable to any other challenge that comes our way, making us stronger. Keep shifting, learning, and overcoming. It's a process—and it's beautiful.

THE FOUNDATION

With a strong foundation, a house is secure. The house will be more resistant to intrusion of cold or moisture, and it will resist movement of the earth around it. If the foundation is not stable, walls may crack, doors may not operate properly, floors may slope, and if there is moisture intrusion, mold may grow and spread. This is something that homeowners and buyers are typically very concerned about.

However when it comes to our own foundation as people, we sometimes ignore it. We just start building our lives, careers, family, relationships, and activities with no thought about our foundation. This can happen because the world screams that speed is important, and the easy road is the best road. But the loud messages we receive from our culture are rarely true. The truth often seems counterintuitive, difficult, and painful and looks like hard work. But if we operate in a fantasy, we will never have stability and true success in our lives.

It's important to face reality, however difficult this may be. Maybe we had a great upbringing and supportive family, with minimal issues, and our foundation is fine. We may even have a great relationship with God, and our foundation is solid. But if we've had relationship struggles, trauma, or disconnection from God, we can be sure that there are at least cracks in our foundation—or maybe even *no* foundation. Our foundation literally affects everything we try to build in our lives. If we want our prog-ress to be secure and lasting, we have to pay attention to where we need to work on ourselves at a foundational level. If you have a lot of foundational work to do, this section of the book may feel extremely heavy to get through, and it may take you some time.

CONNECTION TO GOD

The best place to start your work is to consider what you believe about God. Unfortunately there is a lot of confusion in our world about who God is. People with the best of intentions may mislead us or misinform us. That is why it's best not only to read the Bible for ourselves but also to engage in a personal relationship with God. The more we get to know God, the more we understand how loving, wise, and capable He is.

Reading the Bible can seem daunting, but the more you read it, the more it draws you in. Just like a baby starts with milk and works its way up to digesting food, you may have to start small. I personally started with daily devotional books that had a verse or two of scripture and some commentary to think about then grad-uated to reading a verse in the book of Psalms or Proverbs directly out of the Bible each day. An easy step from there is to start read-ing a chapter at a time from each New Testament gospel. There are many "Bible in a year" reading plans out there, and when you feel ready, it's a great way to get through the entire Bible. I have read the Bible several times now, and it continually deepens my understanding of who God is and who I am. There are so much love and wisdom packed into this book, and every time you read it, you will learn something new, even if you are rereading some-thing you've already read several times. That is why it is called the "living word of God." It is incredible and something you have to experience to understand.

In addition to reading the Bible, it's important to find ways to communicate with God and develop a prayer life if you do not already have one. Thankfully, even if we do not do the best job of expressing ourselves in prayer, God sees each of us clearly and at all times. Nothing about us is a surprise to Him, and He loves us. He sees strength in each of us that He wants us to see in ourselves and does not want us to suffer. He wants us to let go of our fears and embrace Him because He is where we find hope. However, it can be frustrating if we do not know how to communicate with God.

We know what it takes to have a good conversation with someone we care about, and the same principles are true when having a conversation with God. Just like any genuine personal relationship that we cultivate, like a marriage or a close friendship, things go better when we are open and honest and listen fully to the other person. No one wants to feel that you are trying to follow a strict script, to follow certain rules, or to be someone you are not. We want true connection, and we want people to approach us in a genuine and relaxed way. Even if our favorite people are not perfect, not eloquent in their words, or are quirky in presentation, it does not change how much we enjoy spending time with them. Unique, imperfect people make life interesting, fun, and colorful.

In the same way, when we come to God in prayer, we don't have to come to Him in a formal, particular, or polished way. God our Father is creative and delights in differences. He loves intelligence and humor and is not startled by the full range of our emotions. We see this love of variety in His creation, not only in that He created every person to be unique. But look at how many species there are of every animal and plant, every variety in landscape, and the changing weather. He wants to know us personally and have a real relationship with us. He wants to hear what we are grateful for, *and* He wants to hear us grumble about what is not going well. And once we've laid it all at His feet, He wants to speak to us and share His love and wisdom.

God tells us that when we seek Him, we find Him. When we ask, we receive. But often, the thing we need the most, the *real* answer to our problems, is the thing we continuously run away from. We prefer to talk *to* Him and avoid conversation *with* Him. We avoid the wisdom He provides. Most have heard this saying by the Greek philosopher Epictetus: "We have two ears and one mouth so we can listen twice as much as we speak." In every relationship we truly should listen more than we speak, and the same goes for our relationship with God. He is the all-knowing Creator of the universe who personally crafted *you* in your mother's womb, so He probably knows a thing or two.

Why do we avoid hearing from God at times, avoid what we know deep down is true? We could be afraid of being let down or of hearing something we don't want to hear. We may think we are unworthy or incapable of hearing directly from God. Or maybe we are afraid of getting what we truly want. Sometimes we are so attached to our difficulties that we don't want to let go of them, even though we know that we must drop the baggage we are carrying in order to grasp the healing, happiness, connection, fulfillment, and all of the things we long for the most (Luke 11:1–13).

If you do not have a good prayer life and an intimate relationship with God, it is important to get to the bottom of it. Thinking about your conversations with God, consider each of these questions carefully. Taking time to pray and journal, or to discuss these with others, will help you flesh out your thoughts and understand yourself better.

- Are you avoiding a relationship with God? If so …
  - What do you believe is making you avoid Him?
  - What is holding you back from prayer?
  - In what ways could this relationship replace unsteadiness in your life with strength?
- How often do you communicate with God?

- How do you best connect with God?
    - o Is it in a particular environment or setting?
    - o Do you do anything in particular while praying, like writing in a journal, listening to music, or going for a walk?
- Do you express gratitude?
- Do you tell God what you need and what you are struggling with?
- Do you feel that the conversation is one-sided, or do you truly listen for God's response?
- What do you think is going well in your prayer life? Why are you grateful for this?
- What could you do to improve your time in prayer and make it more meaningful?
- Do you sense that a stronger prayer life would improve your personal and professional life? How?

There are many ways to engage in prayer, and many ways we will hear from God. Sometimes He speaks to us using a quiet whisper or a gentle nudge, through a touching message at church, a song, through conversation with a friend, or through an experience. He is creative, and we should stay open with expectation for his messages. As you engage prayerfully with the lessons in this book, keep your ears and eyes open for God. He will meet you where you are. Here are some of my personal prayer practices that may be helpful for you:

- Praying, reading the Bible, and discussing insights with my husband every morning as we drink coffee is the best part of my day. We have been doing this for years, and we learn a lot from this time together.
- I love finding cozy, little chapels where I can pray. My favorite is a small chapel with a big, lifelike picture of Jesus

right in the middle of the room, surrounded by flickering candles. It is so comforting and a great place for quiet prayer and reflection.

- Often when I go for a run or a walk, I will set a prayer intention. This is a great way to waken my spirit while engaging in physical activity, and I often get great insights during this time.
- Choosing a day every now and then to engage in several hours of silence, with no technology, and maybe even while fasting, can be a powerful time. Eliminating distractions in this way allows me to hear from God more clearly. I've had some great breakthroughs during times like this.
- Journaling is a regular practice for me. It's evolved from writing about what I'm frustrated about, what I'm grateful for, or what happened in my day, to writing down my prayers and freewriting an answer from God. This took me a while to master because it's difficult to quiet your own thoughts and let the Holy Spirit speak through the pen to the paper. It's even harder to write down things that come to your mind without judgment, even when they seem weird. But I've gotten some really great insights when doing this. While I'm sure my own mind sometimes takes over and gets in the way, I am positive that I regularly hear from the Holy Spirit.
- It took us a long time to find a great church where we feel that the Holy Spirit speaks to us every single week. I would highly encourage you to try different churches and find a place where you hear God speaking to you through the messages.
- Joining a Bible-study group can be a great place to deepen your faith through study and conversation with others.

TRUE IDENTITY

Oftentimes we want to focus on our current situations and put our past behind us. We may do this because we feel it's not relevant, it's painful, or we want to dismiss the cheesy notion peddled by psychologists that we all have a child within us needing our attention. We are grown up and believe we need to focus on grown-up things to make the most of our time. The problem with this is that our childhood shapes who we are. Many of our thoughts and behaviors are so deeply rooted within us from childhood that they are automatic. Of course, there may be many positive experiences and lessons that we carry into adulthood. However, negative experiences from our childhood often undermine what we are trying to achieve in life. This is because many of our beliefs and behaviors are programmed on childhood fear, misconceptions, or dysfunction. They work in our subconscious, and unless we are intentional about uncovering them, we cannot root them out. These unevaluated parts of ourselves lead to stormy situations in our minds and hearts as time goes by and can literally affect every area of our lives.

The best way to identify false beliefs rooted in childhood is by learning the truth about who we are. There are many places in the Bible that tell us about our *true* identity, and I would encourage you to spend time reading the Bible *every* day. The more time you spend in God's word, digesting it, the more it will saturate you with truth. Over time, you become more discerning and can more easily pinpoint things that are stealing the freedom and peace God gave you.

In a time of prayer and reflection, God led me to write down a list of feelings that I was experiencing. God then led me to write His responses to each feeling without looking at what the first list said. When I read the statements side by side, I was amazed at how each one fit perfectly. I believe that God shares this insight for anyone who is seeking Him and trying to learn more about who you actually are. As you read through each of these, take a little time to think about what it means to feel a certain way at times, and contrast this with who God says you *truly* are. Think about how it feels to embrace the identity God has given you. Then go through the list again while considering how you treat the people in your life. It can be healing to see others in the way God does and to treat them in a way that helps them see who they really are in Christ.

What You May Feel/ Believe about Yourself	God's Response to You
Unsupported	Justified
Unseen	Redeemed
Unimportant	Worthy, treasured
Unheard, uncared for	Loved beyond measure
Not Valuable	Valued
Forgotten	Esteemed
Unworthy, without purpose	Crowned in righteousness
Don't belong	Beloved
Dysfunctional	Immortal
Bad person, wasted effort	Forever mine, claimed
Unloved	Adopted
Invisible	Lifted
Beneath others	Praised
Rejected	Adored
Lost	Protected
Lonely	Sanctified (set aside for God)
Orphaned	Holy
Stray, alone, different	One with me
Trash	Chosen
Barely hanging on (scarcely enough)	Special (surpassing what is common, distinct among others)

- Do any of these feelings or beliefs resonate with you? Why?
- Does God's word match what you currently believe about yourself and what you are experiencing?
  - In what specific ways?
  - How do you know?
- Do you believe what God says to be true about you, or is there a disconnect?
  - Where did the belief come from?
  - Is there anything in your upbringing or current life that may be reinforcing an incorrect belief about who you are?
- Who does God say that you are, and what does He say you should be experiencing in life?
- When will you know that you have embraced God's thoughts about you?
- How will your personal and professional life look/feel different when you believe that what God says is true about you?
- What are some specific actions you can take to help someone in your life believe what God says to be true about them?

If you identify a disconnect, this is a wonderful opportunity because you can work to turn this thought pattern around. You can process the experiences, thoughts, and feelings you have and work toward clarity and a proper mindset. This can be done through prayer, with a counselor, writing in your journal, discussing with your group, or any other way that works for you. Some things you can quickly come to terms with, while other things will take time and effort. Be patient with yourself, and know that God will bring you the answers and healing that you need. Don't forget to celebrate the ways you are living in alignment with who you truly are! This is where you feel satisfied and complete.

HEALING TRAUMA

Whether the trauma is from your childhood, or from your recent past, this is something that needs attention and healing. Traumatic experiences are like dark shadows that live in us during times of distress and often make their home in our minds and hearts. Later in life, when they creep into our awareness, we may think they are just a nuisance that we need to swat away. However, they are actually working in our subconscious minds to diminish or destroy any good that we are working toward in our life. They dull experiences that should be vibrant and joyful, ruin connection with others, stop us from doing things we are called to do, and drain our energy as we consciously or unconsciously struggle to overcome them.

Shadows don't live in light, and the only way to get rid of them is to temporarily shift the light of our focus on them. We need to shine our attention into every dark corner of our spirit in search of the truth and find anything that may be hiding in the background. When we invite God into these shadow investigations, He protects us from the negativity that is stirred up and helps us sort through it in a healthy way. We should examine what we find just long enough to unpack the pain and limiting beliefs that the issues carry and long enough to forgive ourselves and others for these unwanted guests. And once we *deal with* the pain, we are *free!*

- Have you experienced trauma in your life? What did you experience?
- How did these experiences affect you at the time?
- Do you feel that these experiences still affect you in big or small ways? Explain.
- Which experience do you think affects you the most and should be addressed first?

- Who or what can support you in healing from this experience (e.g., prayer, counselor, friend, spouse, coach, and book/podcast)?
- How will your life look different when you no longer struggle with the aftershock of trauma?
- Will healing this past trauma change your personal or business relationships? How?

QUALITY PEOPLE

It sounds fantastic to be surrounded by a crowd of family and friends who are amazing, supportive, and make us happy. But the truth is if we don't have the right people in our lives and invite anyone in without discretion, we can become overwhelmed with problems and frustrations or even feel lonely in the midst of the people around us. Loneliness makes the heart sick, and if you are lonely right now, either because you do not have support or because you are surrounded by the wrong people, I am hopeful that the things you are learning here will pull you out of that dark, draining feeling.

I am a believer that we should focus on *quality* over quantity. If you currently have very few or maybe no supportive people in your life, think of this as your opportunity to rebuild on a good solid foundation. Be thoughtful and selective about the people you involve in your life. God sets boundaries, and so should you! When we are selective about who is allowed into our inner circle, the people we trust the most to share our lives with, we find fulfillment in our relationships.

Even the more superficial relationships we engage in should be carefully evaluated for quality. If you allow someone who does not belong into your life, they could be a curse to you and rob you of the peace and joy God wants for you. There is no perfect person, but there are those who bring mostly good things into our lives—like encouragement, laughter, support, and positive influence.

We only have a limited amount of time and energy so we should use it wisely and spend time with the people who elevate and magnify the good in our lives. We can also choose to work with the people in our lives to create healthier relationships. However, it's important to consider that we can only do our part. If others don't want to participate in our lives in a positive and meaningful way, it is their choice. When someone can't maintain their end of the relationship in a positive way, it's not about you. "Hurt people hurt people." We may not be able to change others, but we can choose who we allow into our lives or to what degree. There is no need to settle for less than what God wants for us.

- Who do you value in your life? Why?
- Who brings positivity and joy into your life? Why? (Write down each name, and journal about each person and the relationship you have with them.)
- Do you have any relationships that you should reevaluate? Why? (Write down each name, and journal about each person and the relationship you have with them.)
    o Do you think that the relationship could be beneficial and positive with some work?
    o Do you think the other person would be receptive to making adjustments so that the relationship is healthy?
- Do you have any unmet relationship needs? What specifically do you need?
    o Is there anyone that you know that could fill them?
    o If not, where can you meet someone to fulfill the need?

- How would more positive relationships in your life make you more successful in your personal and professional life?

PROPER ALIGNMENT

There is always an order to things in maintaining stability in the foundation as well as in what is built above it. God *is love* and He should be our foundation. Anything He commands us to do is because He loves us and wants good for us. The most important commandments that God gave us are *first* to love the Lord God with all your heart and with all your soul and with all your mind. The *second* is to love your neighbor *as* yourself. This means we put God first, then people. And loving people includes *yourself.* It does not say to love people and forget about yourself. It says, "Love your neighbor as yourself." When things are out of order spiritually, our lives become messes. Think about a delicious cake recipe that you like to make. What if you did things out of order or mixed up the ingredients? What if you simply added salt instead of sugar? Maybe you just left out the baking soda? Can you spread frosting on your cake before you bake it? Needless to say, none of this works. Proper alignment with God's order brings order to your life. God's ways may take time and work, and getting ourselves in the proper order may take a little thought, but the result from following His recipe doesn't disappoint! His ways are always simple, and His wisdom can be easily applied from one situation to another.

- Are you currently in alignment by putting your relationship with God first and with people and yourself second?
    - o   How does that affect your personal life?
    - o   How does it affect your professional life?

- Are you loving yourself in the same way you love others?
  - How does that affect your personal life?
  - How does it affect your professional life?
- What practical changes can you make in your daily life that will ensure that you are in alignment?
- What positive differences will you see in your life when you are in alignment?
- If you are already in alignment, what benefits does this bring to your life?

PLUMBING

The plumbing, electrical, heating, and air-conditioning systems are vitally important in your home. These are systems that make the home functional and comfortable. Buyers will insist on fixing them if they are not up to par. As a person and real estate agent, your mind, heart, and spirit/soul are your major systems. With any one of these functioning poorly, your quality of life and your ability to be productive and successful will be lessened.

When thinking about plumbing in a house, we want our houses consistently to allow the flow of good clean water into our homes and eliminate the unwanted waste from our homes. This is a critical system, working in two directions simultaneously.

When our plumbing is working properly, we have control over turning the water on or off. We can also flush unwanted waste out of our home by deciding to do so. When our plumbing is not functioning properly, we may not be getting the proper flow of water into our home, and we are unable to flush waste out. We could even have leaks that prevent us from controlling the flow of water and damage the house.

FLOW OF THOUGHTS

The plumbing system represents the flow of our thoughts in both our personal and professional lives. There are thoughts that are good and refreshing to us, helping us feel alive and productive. We want these to flow in! Anything that is negative and destructive, sapping our productivity, we want out! We must be intentional and take action to continually direct this, just like we are when we turn the faucet on and off or when we flush the toilet.

If you think about it, our thoughts are either the refreshing water or the toxic waste, continually with us throughout our days, weeks, months, years, and literally our entire lives. Second Corinthians 10:5 tells us to "take every thought captive." This means that we need to recognize each thought, examine it, and determine if it is acceptable and in alignment with God or if it is a destructive thought. We are not victims of our thoughts, and we have the power to turn the faucet on further or to shut it off. What we do with our thoughts can create huge advantages or disadvantages in life because wherever our attention goes, so do our actions.

In essence, your thoughts affect every part of your life! If, for example, you are continually worrying about your spouse leaving you, you will bring destruction to your relationship because this thought will influence your behavior. You may be more self-absorbed, fearful, and needy. However, if you are thinking more about how you can love your spouse, your relationship will be infused with life because you will be thinking and acting in a loving way, strengthening the relationship.

In your professional life, when you are concerned about market conditions or where your next commission will come from, this will influence your behavior and you may be pushier and more self-absorbed. This will turn clients off and have a negative impact on your business. However, when your focus is on the opportunity to serve them and help them achieve their goals, your behavior changes. You are not worried about your commission, and you act in a more loving way. You listen more carefully, and you bring them real solutions that are based on *their* needs, not yours. This ultimately leads to connection with your client, and a successful outcome.

You will build success or sabotage your success, depending on the condition of your mind and the quality of your thoughts. Philippians 4 gives us a guide on how to think. The author, Paul, tells us that we should practice gratitude, and rather than feeling anxious or worried, we should put our trust in God and pray for His help. Our thoughts should be focused on what is true, honorable, just, pure, lovely, commendable, excellent, and praiseworthy.

Additionally, we need an optimistic mindset, knowing that everything is possible through Christ Jesus, who brings supernatural fruitfulness in the things you pursue. He truly works *all* things for good when we are working in His will and purpose for us. The things that He works for good include mistakes, shortcomings, things that seem unrelated, big things, small things, and all things. When you know this, you understand that optimism should not be "faking it till you make it." Instead, it is a solid truth that you can anchor yourself to.

When we discipline our minds to think about the right things, we don't have room for destructive thoughts that weigh us down. We can operate in confidence, knowing that God is our ultimate provider and that when we are in alignment with Him and His will, He fulfills the desires of our hearts and gives us what we need in any given situation.

"Our mind is a garden; our thoughts are the seeds. We can grow flowers, or we can grow weeds." This clever quote is a great illustration of what happens in our mind. While weeds or negative thoughts will spread when unattended, we have the power to stop them and proactively to plant the healthy flowers and thoughts that we want to grow. It is helpful to apply this to any and every area of our lives because any of our thoughts in one area lead to thoughts in other areas. We only have one mind that we carry into *all* situations, so we must make sure that we are tending our thoughts as they relate to God and our relationships with family and friends, ourselves, our personal lives, and our professional lives.

When our thoughts are in alignment with God's will, we are considering first what God wants, and we are also holding everyone's needs as important. An example would be praying for the greater good and for every person involved in a real estate transaction to experience success—including the buyers, sellers, the agent on the other side of the transaction, our third-party vendors, and ourselves. We recognize that there are certain things we can control, and other things that only God can handle. We can focus on our part without worrying about the bigger picture because we know God is active. We believe that God is working all things for good so we are able to let go of outcomes and be more flexible.

- What healthy thought patterns do you engage in?
  - How do these help you to be successful in your personal and professional life?
- What unhealthy thought patterns do you have?
  - Are these thoughts usually directed at certain people or a certain area of your life?
  - How do these thoughts make you feel?
  - Are you aware of how these thoughts affect other things in your life?
  - How would you like to think differently?
- What are some practical things you can do to change your attitudes and/or your thinking?
- How will healthier thoughts affect your personal and professional life?
- How will healthier thoughts benefit the individual people around you?

FAITH OR FEAR

The plumbing system also represents the flow of our faith into our personal and professional lives and the flushing out of our fears. Faith and fear can be expressed in so many ways! Many agents struggle with the fear of rejection because they do not realize how much value they bring to their clients. Fear is a huge distraction that keeps us from being productive. Faith is the antidote to fear. We may have many talents and skills that we bring to the table, and when we also bring the power of God, we are unstoppable. This is where we draw strength and confidence. On our own, we are flawed, imperfect, and limited. With God we have unlimited knowledge, wisdom, and strength revealed to us through the Holy Spirit. We should always show up for our clients with optimism, expecting good things to happen. We can do this because God is good, and when we allow Him to work through us, He works all things for good. Even when things are not going according to our plan, we know that God has a better plan. While we may not understand why things are unfolding in the way they are, through faith we can comfortably move forward as God guides us through His process to accomplish His will.

Maybe we aren't struggling with rejection. Maybe our struggle with embracing our value is because we somehow feel that it is inappropriate. Or perhaps we have been taught by family or friends to hide our talents from the world so that we do not seem conceited or greedy or stand out from the crowd. Some people are afraid of success and self-actualization, and they project this false reality onto others.

> Our deepest fear is not that we are inadequate. Our deepest fear is that we are powerful beyond measure. It is our light, not our darkness, that most frightens us. We ask ourselves, Who am

I to be brilliant, gorgeous, talented, fabulous? Actually, who are you not to be? You are a child of God. Your playing small doesn't serve the world. There's nothing enlightened about shrinking so that other people won't feel insecure around you. We are all meant to shine, as children do. (Marianne Williamson)

Another reason we can feel deficient in value is due to comparison. When we compare ourselves to others, we diminish our individuality and our unique gifts. Just because one person is a successful real estate agent, due to their strong ability in one area, does not mean that every other real estate agent can't be immensely successful using their own strengths in a combination of other areas. Use what you've got. It's valuable!

- Do you ever struggle with fears of rejection?
    - When and how does it show up for you?
- How do you behave when you are fearing rejection?
    - What is the root of your fear (e.g., that you will be unlovable, disrespected, or left behind)?
    - Where did this fear come from?
- Have you been given the message that playing it small is more acceptable than going for your dreams in any area of your life?
    - How does this affect you personally and professionally?
- Do you struggle with comparison?
    - Who do you typically compare yourself to?
    - How does this make you feel?
- What will it look like when you value your unique gifts, talents, and wisdom?
    - How will it affect the people around you?

    o   How will you show up differently in your personal and professional life?

It's important to remember that our family, friends, and clients are also all in a battle to keep the flow of good coming into their lives and flushing out the bad. There are always ways that you can support them in this. When thinking of our clients, here is an example of how we might help them untangle their fears.

Have you ever had to untangle something? Think about a string of Christmas lights, a long mane of horse hair, or yarn that has unraveled and then gotten tangled up. Untangling something takes attention, finesse, and patience. It is not easy to do, but as you work at it, it gets easier, and when you have completed the task, it is very satisfying. This is what we have to do for our clients at times.

There is a lot of mental and emotional energy that goes into buying or selling a home. No matter how great a job we as agents do to set proper expectations and be proactive in our transactions, it is inevitable that some thoughts will be tangled along the way. Clients may receive input from their families and friends, and this input can be riddled with fears and misconceptions. They may be juggling a lot of priorities and feel overwhelmed by the process. There could be stress about finances or family disagreements. All of these things can create obstacles to their getting what they really want. It's our job to notice this and help them.

As their guide, when we notice that they are getting tangled, we can stop and give them our attention. We can ask questions about what they are experiencing and provide some clarity and guidance that will help them untangle. It may take a little time to get them to open up to share their thoughts and fears with us, but once they do, we will gain momentum in helping them find solutions and relief. Of course we need to use discernment to stay within the boundaries of our position while also having the courage to work through tangles that may not be directly related to the transaction but attached to their personal lives.

One great way to do this with our clients is to start with highlighting their original goal or objective. Talk about this, and then transition into the reality of the situation. Discuss what they are facing and what challenges and feelings they are experiencing. Once you know this, you can discuss all of the options and possibilities for finding a resolution. Let them choose what works best, and then guide them forward, free of tangles and free of fear.

CONTROL AND SURRENDER

The balance between control and surrender is a skill that every real estate agent needs to learn. There are many ways that we practice this. It is in working with our clients to help them choose the right home, negotiating with the other parties in the transaction, dealing with market conditions, with seasonality, and even with our own aptitudes and shortcomings. While in other examples we've considered what we want to flow in and what we want to flush out as it relates to plumbing, here we want to take hold of the things within our control and release the tight grip we have on things we cannot control.

Have you ever been in a situation or a season of life where you felt ill-equipped for the monumental challenge in front of you? A situation where you wish there were some kind of instruction manual or an easy way through it but you knew there wasn't? We all face situations like this in both small and massive ways as we go through life. How do we respond to them? We can get overwhelmed and freeze, we can run away from the challenge, or we can look the challenge dead in the eye and start moving forward one step at a time, with the confidence that somehow we will make it, figuring it out as we go. This is a great approach—as long as we remember that we cannot control everything.

In each challenge we face, as we do what we can, we can be sure that God can handle the rest. If we invite God into the situation, we will have everything we need. He guides us through our challenges step by step and gets us to the place where we can round the corner, overcoming that challenge, and moving into something new. He typically doesn't let us see what is around the corner before we get there, but as we round the corner, we see that He knew exactly where He was taking us, and we see that it is good.

He loves each of us immensely and wants us to get through our challenges with victory. Our role is to listen, trust, and take action as He lovingly guides us. He never intended for us to do it on our own, and He wants to be with us through it all.

Finding the balance between control and surrender includes grounding ourselves in the present moment, where we are free of fear and judgment. More than anything, it is trusting that God has a plan that is bigger than any of us can see or understand. We must pray for His will in every transaction and for every person involved, including agents, buyers, sellers, and third-party participants.

When we truly believe that God is in charge, that He is truly loving and wise, it takes the pressure off us as agents. We are no longer the pushy salespeople trying to force a specific outcome. We are instruments of God's goodness and love serving the people around us as we are guided by the Holy Spirit. Even when it doesn't seem to make sense, we continue following the prompts we receive from the Holy Spirit, and things unfold in the best way possible.

> God grant me the serenity to accept the things
> I cannot change, courage to change the things
> I can, and the wisdom to know the difference,

living one day at a time; enjoying one moment at a time; taking this world as it is and not as I would have it; trusting that You will make all things right if I surrender to Your will; so that I may be reasonably happy in this life and supremely happy with You forever in the next. Amen. (Reinhold Niebuhr)

- How well do you stay in the present moment?
    - o What gets in your way?
    - o When are you at your best?
- Do you feel that you work in a proper balance of control and surrender?
    - o Why? Or why not?
- In what ways do you excel in taking control of situations?
- In what ways do you excel in surrendering when needed?
- Do you feel that you need to work on the process of control and surrender in any area of your life?
    - o In what ways do you need to improve?
    - o What can you do to maintain a better balance?
    - o In what ways are you already succeeding, and how does this benefit your life?

HVAC

Your heating, ventilation, and air-conditioning system, or HVAC system, controls heating and cooling in your home and works to improve air quality. You cannot see your air quality or the temperature, but they are critical and directly impact your comfort and your health. This invisible system represents your spirit and soul, two intangible qualities that are critical to every person.

SPIRIT AND SOUL

Your *spirit* is where hope, love, and faith live. This is also your character, integrity, and perseverance. Your *soul* is your overall character and your unique combination of attributes. This could include your mind, heart, will, thoughts, desires, and anything intangible that makes you who you are. It's hard to tell the difference between your spirit and your soul because they overlap and intersect in ways that are hard to identify. For example, think about how a horse compares with a lion. The traits we typically associate with a horse are that it is independent, free, noble, enduring, confident, and triumphant. A lion typically embodies traits like courage, power, strength, and leadership. Every type of animal is unique in its purpose and its intangible qualities, and each individual animal, even within the same species, still has its own unique personality.

When we bring our gifts into the world, it can sometimes feel discouraging when we think of competing with so many others offering the same services. However, this is an illusion. We are not competing at all because there are no two people who are the same. We all have unique traits, talents, abilities, and experience. There is a need for us to serve the world in our own unique way.

With that being said, it is important to keep in mind that our soul and spirit are not fixed. They are flowing. We need continually to assess where we are and where we want to go in our development. Again, remember that each of us has infinite potential! Go with the flow of who you are and who you are becoming. You can do both by practicing acceptance of who you are, having a vision of who you want to be, and staying flexible and intentional as you move forward.

- Are you prone to comparison?
  - Who do you typically compare yourself to, and why?
  - How does it make you feel?
- What are some attributes that are uniquely combined to make you who you are?
  - How does it make you feel that these attributes represent you?
  - Is there anything you want to develop within yourself or strengthen?
  - Are there any traits you want to lean into more and emphasize more in your life?
- Are you embracing the person you are?
  - Do you recognize your unique qualities and how they benefit the people around you?

  o   How can you express your individuality more in
      the things you do?
  o   How do you think embracing your individuality
      can reduce comparison of yourself to others?

TRUE SUCCESS

Embracing our individuality also means accepting God's unique
plan and purpose for each of us. This is why it's important to
turn to God as we develop into who we were meant to be and for
guidance in everything we do. Sometimes we can get useful suggestions from people in our lives who have the best of intentions
for us, but the reality is that they are imperfect, seeing things from
their unique perspective and with limited wisdom. They might
tell you to turn back from something you started because it's too
complicated to reach your destination, when in reality you have
what it takes to accomplish your goal. They may give you the
wrong directions and you end up feeling completely lost.

God wants us to learn to trust Him in the process He is taking us through. God is all-knowing and all-powerful. When He
directs you to do something, He is continually by your side and
you cannot go wrong when taking His guidance. Even if you
make mistakes along the way, He will be with you, no matter how
many times you screw up. Just like the GPS system in your car,
He continually redirects you when you make a wrong turn. You
are not alone.

Instead of depending on friends, family, or colleagues to help
you make decisions or work through problems, turn to God.
Sometimes God does speak to us through people, but we should
go to Him for confirmation because we need the truth from Him.
He provides all we need in every circumstance, and we can depend

on Him regardless of our shortcomings. He makes us wise and shows us where to go.

The people around us may have good intentions for us when telling us where to go with our life plans. They just want us to be happy and successful. However, let's explore the meaning of *true success* and how our individuality matters. When we are born, we are naturally joyful. As babies, we squeal and laugh in delight even though we are limited in what we can do. We do not base our joy on our production or on any predetermined level or type of success. We are simply in a state of joy.

As adults, sometimes we can get caught up in what success means to others, and we can start chasing after the wrong things. We feel the pressures of the responsibility and external standards that are imposed on us, and this makes it difficult to stay connected to that feeling of joy. The world may tell us that we should all be the same, but this does not work. Imagine a bird trying to be a tiger. It will never be a successful tiger because it was made to be a bird. When trying to roar, it would sing a pleasant song. When trying to leap, it would fly. Trying to attain success in a way that is not meant for us can drain our energy, taking us away from the things we really want in life and from all of the things that are possible for us as individuals.

God has programmed each of us with seeds of greatness, and in the right conditions, these seeds spring to life and grow. We must allow God to show us who we are and allow His process to develop within us in the special way He intended for each of us. When we do this, we take control back and do not allow external messages and demands to drive us. We can simply be who we are, performing at our best in the way we were intended to, gaining achievement, satisfaction, joy, and true success.

It's important to take a step back from everything we are trying to achieve and to think about what success really means to us as individuals.

- Are you living from the place of your unique purpose?
- How are you using your individual gifts and abilities to serve the world around you?
- What activities bring you joy?
- What does success truly mean for you?

ELECTRICAL

The electrical system brings power to our home in an almost magical way. All we have to do is to flip a switch, and we are no longer in the dark. We all want a working electrical system so that we are able to turn on the lights, plug things in, and use our electrical devices to make our lives easier. In the same way, we as people can use our own power to create the lives we want, and this is also pretty magical when you think about it.

DESIRES OF YOUR HEART

The main service panel is like a switchboard for all of the electrical activity in your house. It receives all of the incoming power and distributes it throughout the house. In the same way, one's heart is the starting point to every other activity we initiate in our lives. It is where your deepest desires live and where love flows from. What is the condition of your heart?

> Hope deferred makes the heart sick, but a desire fulfilled is a tree of life. (Proverbs 13:12)

We feel alive and vibrant when pursuing the things that our heart desires. When we "go for it" and step forward into the things we want, it feels amazing. This could simply be jumping into a pool on a warm day or something big like starting a business you've dreamed of for years. It could be getting married to the love of your life, taking that trip you've been longing for, or even just engaging in a hobby you love. It is satisfying, and it brings us joy to do the things we desire, even when there is hard work involved.

Unfortunately there are times when hope is deferred and we forfeit our dreams. This makes us feel lifeless and depressed. The reasons for this happening are more than I can name. We must get to the bottom of what is stopping us. Sometimes it's as simple as a mindset that needs to be shifted, or it could be a long-held belief that needs to be released. It could be fear of rejection, perceived unworthiness, or not embracing our own greatness. Maybe we experienced something difficult in the past and need healing. Whatever is causing this will require our attention and work to identify and remedy it.

Now consider how effectively you are loving. The condition of our heart is also a reflection of how well love is flowing through it and how we are loving God, others, and ourselves. All of these types of love are important, and the hierarchy is key. God first, then loving others as yourself. And please note that it is not *only* loving others or loving them *more* than yourself, but loving others *as* you love yourself. We are *all* important to God. Love is universal, and we are all human beings who need love, made by a Creator who is love. Therefore, love should be flowing in both our personal lives and our professional lives. When our thoughts and actions are loving, connection is possible.

Sometimes when we are practicing real estate, we can become too focused on facts, metrics, market data, or our next sale and forget about love. This is a dangerous imbalance because we cannot achieve anything without love. People buy houses because of love. They want to provide shelter, security, and warmth for their families and their pets. They want a place to call home. They

choose their agents because they feel seen, heard, respected, protected, and ultimately loved by them. If you are not dishing out the
light and love, your business may go dark. The same thing is true
for your personal life. You may lose key relationships if you are not
acting in love. And if you are not giving and receiving love in your
personal life, you will enter your work relationships empty and
have nothing to give. Everything good in life is working through
a cycle of love. So make sure that you are experiencing love in
every area of your life because it will brighten and magnify your
overall life experience.

- Considering the deepest desires of your heart, what are
  you hoping for?
  - What do you want to achieve in your personal life?
  - What do you want to achieve in your professional
    life?
  - Are you actively engaging in the desires of your
    heart?
- Do you feel like love is flowing freely through your heart?
  - How do you feel when operating from a place of
    love?
  - Do you feel like there are any blockages?
  - Where do they show up?
  - What can you do to remove any blockages?
- Are you loving God with all of your heart, mind, and soul?
  How do you know?
- Are you loving others as yourself? How and when?
- Are you loving yourself? How do you practice this?
- How will your life look when you are operating more often
  from a place of love and it is flowing freely?
- What activities do you currently engage in that make you
  feel loving?
  - How do these enhance your life?

Generosity is another element of the way we work through our heart. When we give with some kind of expectation from another person, our lives become transactional, and it takes the joy out of giving and receiving. The person giving feels frustrated and resentful until their expectation is met, and the person receiving feels manipulated and unloved.

True generosity is giving out of a place of love and wanting to connect with another human being. It is choosing to use our time, resources, and love without expectation from anyone. When we operate from this place, we feel satisfied even if we don't get a thank-you from a friend or a client does not take our advice. We see much more happiness and success in our lives when we approach our personal relationships and our clients in this way.

The key to this kind of generosity is maintaining good boundaries. If we do not think that we should engage in something, or we sense that we will feel resentful if we do it, we should say no without reservation and without excuses. This takes practice and is very uncomfortable at first. But as you learn to let your "yes be yes" and your "no be no" (Matthew 5:37), you will find that the people around you will feel joy when you give freely to them and will respect your integrity when you say no. You will be filled with purpose and joy.

- Do you consider yourself a generous person? Why? Or why not?
- Think of a time you gave, expecting to receive something in return. How did this feel for you, and for the other person?
- Think of a time that you have given generously without expecting anything in return. How did it feel? Was it worth the sacrifice involved?
- Are you good at setting boundaries and letting your "yes be yes" and your "no be no"?

- What can you do to improve the boundaries you set?
- How would you like to give more in your personal or professional life?
- How will your life look and feel different as you increase in generosity to those around you?
- Explore a time when you were generous and how it made you and the other person feel.
    - What was the importance of this act?

Finally, let's explore true connection and how this applies to our heart health. True connection with our family, friends, clients, partners, coworkers, and everyone we interact with in a real estate transaction is important. In every area of our lives, we thrive when we are someone whom people like and trust. We become this kind of person by displaying vulnerability, showing others who we truly are, operating out of integrity and honesty, and having a heart for serving others.

Many people try to take shortcuts in building relationships. They talk badly about others to elevate themselves. They are phony, ego-stroking, and pretending to care for the best interests of others. But no one can keep a mask on twenty-four hours a day. And when your words and actions are not coming from a true place, people will at times get a glimpse of who you truly are and will begin to have hesitations about trusting you. If you are not interested in doing the right thing for the people around you, it is time to dig deep and find out where you need healing. Ask God to reveal this to you, to show you why you are not loving others in the way you should. Until you can truly love others, you will not be able to reach your full potential for success at home or at work.

If you feel that you are successfully creating connections with others, ask God to deepen your understanding and ability to connect with others. There is always room to grow, and it is God's true pleasure to elevate you to the next level.

- Who do you experience true connection with in your life?
  - How does it feel when you are connected?
  - Is there any way that you can improve the connection you already feel?
- Who do you experience disconnection with in your life?
  - Is this disconnection a healthy boundary or something that needs work?
  - How does it feel when you are disconnected?
  - What are some practical ways that you can generate connection in this area of your life?
- How will you feel when you are connected in healthy ways to the people in your life?

THINGS YOU BELIEVE

A belief is a subjective attitude that we have about someone or something that we have developed over time. It is more fixed than the transient thoughts we have throughout a day. It is a mindset of faith, trust, or confidence about who or what we are believing. Literally everything we do that creates positive or negative results in our lives starts here. Our beliefs are the operating system program that we execute into thoughts and actions, which ultimately create the life we have. If things are going well, we are likely operating from positive beliefs. If we are unhappy with the state of our lives, chances are that our beliefs are not serving us well. Sometimes we need to revamp our beliefs in order to be successful, productive, and happy.

My mom always used to say, "Where there's a will, there's a way!" and I've found this to be true over and over again in my life. When you truly want something and believe you can achieve it, you typically do! When the odds are stacked against you and things are difficult but you believe you *can*, this is when you get resourceful. You look up information online or in books, talk to experts, come up with a plan, and pray for the Holy Spirit to intervene. When you behave in this way, you feel capable, courageous, and unstoppable. On the other hand, when you are feeling helpless and hopeless, believing that things are out of your reach, you do not even think of all the resources available to you. You give up in your mind, and once you do this, no productive action follows.

If you feel stuck and dissatisfied, it's time to believe in something better. Believe that you were created with a purpose and that God wants good things for you. He has equipped you with numerous strengths and resources. He even provided a written guide that we can use to reprogram our minds into a highly functional operating system. This guide is the Bible! God literally lays out everything we need for an abundant and purposeful life. In Mark 9:23 Jesus says, "All is possible for one who believes." God is capable of everything, and when we look to him for the things we need, believing that He is for us, He helps us.

- What are some positive beliefs you hold?
  - How are they affecting each area of your life?
  - What positive things do you see as a result of these beliefs?
- What are some beliefs that are holding you back from things you want in your life?
  - How do these beliefs make you feel and behave?
  - What can you do to replace these with more supportive beliefs?

WORDS HAVE POWER

The Bible tells us that our words have the power of life and death.

> In the beginning was the Word, and the Word
> was with God, and the Word was God. He was
> in the beginning with God. All things were made
> through him, and without him was not any thing
> that was made. In him was life, and the life was
> the light of men. The light shines in the darkness,
> and the darkness has not overcome it. (John 1:1–5)

The Word empowered the miracle of creation, and it still creates our world in big and small ways. To illustrate this point further, I've found Dr. Masaru Emoto's experiment, where he tested the effect words had on water, to be helpful. In the experiment, he exposed music, written and spoken words, and pictures to water. When the water was examined under a microscope after each exposure, it formed beautiful, crystalline shapes similar to snowflakes for words like *love, happiness,* and *thank-you.* Negative statements, on the other hand, created very unorganized and unsettling-looking formations. In our thoughts and communications with others, we must remember that our human bodies are made up mostly of water. What we think and say to others has an enormous impact on ourselves and on others. We should never be complacent about the words we use because they literally create our lives, spiritually and physically.

- Are you supporting the things you want in your life with your words?
  - Why? Or why not?
- How would you describe the quality of your words in each area of your life?

- What area of your life currently displays the highest quality of words?
    - What are the positive impacts of the way you speak?
- What area of your life needs the most improvement?
    - How can you change your words in a way that will make a positive difference to the quality of your life?
    - How will this change affect others?
    - How will your life look different when the quality of your words improves?

DAILY ACTIVITIES

We naturally manifest our beliefs, thoughts, and words in our daily activities. There is so much we can learn by harnessing this power. It can be far-reaching, into every area of our lives, because our lives are essentially made up of thoughts, words, and behaviors. I am a firm believer that it is always beneficial to learn more on these topics and learn how to apply them to each and every area of your life. Here are just a few examples, but the opportunities are endless.

The first impression we make on the people we meet is one way that we can use our actions to create the life we want. The first impression starts with what someone sees, what they hear you say, the way you connect with them through a smile, handshake, or hug, and how you make them feel. There is a lot to learn here. It's important to learn how to show up in a positive mindset with an intention of what you want to achieve—creating the right image, speaking in a way that is engaging, and with the right body language and words, thus making someone feel the way that you want them to feel. This impression guides what they think of you and starts the relationship rolling in the direction you set it to go in. You truly do have control over this to a great degree.

Another example of an action we can take is meeting with people in person rather than communicating over email or by a text message. Meeting in person may seem to be more time intensive than it's worth. However, it is extremely valuable and worth every minute that it takes to make it happen. Not only do we get to give a fuller message to someone of who we are through the physical impression that we make, but we also learn more about *them*. Statistics show that 70–93 percent of human communication is nonverbal, so choosing to communicate in another way only gives you a small percentage of the information you need. For instance, seeing body language can confirm or contradict what someone is saying. If someone is not being honest with their words, their body will tell you the truth because the message from their body will not match what they are saying. Being able to see this gives you the opportunity to ask some clarifying questions to get to the bottom of what the person is really thinking or feeling. If this conversation is through text, you have to go with what they write, and this may not be enough.

The final example I will share is about using the tools we already have. When we suddenly feel stuck in life, sometimes it's because we've forgotten about tools and techniques that we've learned in the past. Those same tools are still there for us, but maybe we aren't realizing that we can use them again in this new situation. We can look back at things we've accomplished in the past and how we achieved them then determine if some of the same methods will work in the current situation. That being said, for a tool to be useful, it must be put to use. It takes energy and effort to find it, dust it off, and begin the work. This may seem like a strange statement, but the truth is that we often *think* we are *doing* something because we are *thinking* about what a great idea it is, but in reality we are not actually *doing* it. Thinking about something effective must move from a belief to words and then move to action in order to be useful. Once we have discovered a method that works in things we regularly encounter, we should create a new habit to keep the good results lighting up our world.

- What are some actions you regularly take in each area of your life that are helpful?
  - How did you decide that they would be worth the effort?
  - Why do you think these actions are beneficial?
- What are some things you've been thinking about doing but haven't actually engaged in?
  - How can you get in the right mindset to take action?
  - How do you think these actions will positively affect your life?

THE ROOF

The roof covers the house and protects its interior against unfavorable weather conditions. It also provides stability to the walls, foundation, and the overall structure of the house. When the roof is in good condition, the pouring rain flows nicely off the angled sides outside, while inside the house you remain dry and unaffected, along with everything you care about.

HIGH STANDARDS

The roof represents our overall values. God explicitly tells us that the righteous are ultimately protected and favored. Righteousness is the quality of behaving in a way that is pleasing to God. When we operate in righteousness, we are protected by our wise and loving actions. We can hold our heads high rather than leak or crumble, without negative consequences or shame. Just as we may walk through our neighborhood admiring houses that are architecturally beautiful and well-maintained, we are looked upon by others with favor when our standards for integrity are high.

If we have a weak or leaking roof, when things get difficult, we may compromise our values. When we operate out of unrighteousness or poor morality, we compromise everything that we have worked hard to build. Our lives spiral into complication and chaos when we do not face situations with wisdom, honesty, integrity, good intentions, and self-discipline.

Sometimes it's hard to do the right things when there are options that seem easier or choices that are more valued by the people around us. However, doing the right things will always give us a secure roof over our heads—one that is solid, secure, and proudly pointing above to heaven. When we live our values, the people looking at us see a glimpse of our Heavenly Father, who is all-knowing, all-powerful, and supremely good. They see someone who can be trusted because we point to God's goodness. And we can sit securely under the covering of our righteousness.

- When have you made choices or engaged in actions that damaged the secure covering of your roof?
- When have you made choices or engaged in actions that upheld the strength and security of your roof?
- What habits do you engage in that support the integrity of your personal and professional life?
- Where can you improve your behavior so that you are in alignment with spiritual and physical laws and with commitments you have made to yourself and others?

HONESTY

An agent's reputation is so important! We depend on positive word of mouth and online survey reviews to bring us new clients. However, if we are so worried about what people say about us, this can block us from having the hard conversations that are necessary to move our clients in the right direction.

For example, if we are afraid to upset a seller by telling them they need to clean and declutter their house before putting it on the market, they will not be able to make as much from their sale, and they may stay on the market longer or may not be able to get the house sold at all. Your seller wants to get their house sold for top dollar as quickly as possible. In order to achieve this, they need to hear the truth. Providing the truth is always the righteous behavior that provides security in the long run.

Integrity should always be our focus rather than worrying about what people think of us. Operating from a place of integrity is difficult but rewarding! This is how we truly earn trust and accolades from the people we work with.

> Vulnerability sounds like truth and feels like cour-
> age. Truth and courage aren't always comfortable,
> but they're never weakness. (Brené Brown)

Of course, this also applies to our personal lives. Families and friends can at times make us feel that we should say or do certain things in order to earn their love. But true love only happens when we are allowing others to see who we truly are. We should always aim for honest communication. This is where the treasures in our lives come from. Everything else is counterfeit.

- Do you worry about what your clients, family members, or friends think of you?
  - o What kinds of situations bring this up for you?
  - o Why do you worry about what they think?
- What kinds of people-pleasing behaviors do you engage in when worrying about what others think of you in your personal and professional life?
  - o Are these behaviors bringing about a positive or a negative outcome for you? Why?
- What can you do to embrace honesty with everyone in your life?
- How will it change your life to be more courageous in speaking the truth?

SERVING WITH HUMILITY

God does not tell us to run around exhausting ourselves by seeking people to help and things to do. But when someone asks us for a basic need, or we notice it, we should fulfill it. We can be sure that if we are the person who is seeing a need, we are the person to address it.

We should be humble and willing to help the people around us. This means that we are willing to use our energy and resources, engaging in the discomfort of getting the job done. With that humility, we should also be willing to stretch ourselves beyond our usual job description or what we are comfortable doing. When we are outside our comfort zone, we need to remember that God provides us with everything we need to do good for the people around us. We may not be confident in our own ability, but we can be confident that God is with us and will give us the tools we need to get the job done.

A professional example of serving the people around us would be meeting with a prospective seller about a house that is unusual and will be difficult to sell. We should work to understand their needs and help them achieve their goals in the best way possible. This is not a time for self-doubt, which is self-focused. This is a time for humility as we focus on serving the seller. When God calls us to do something, using the gifts and resources He has given us, we can be sure that He will provide wisdom, tools, and guidance as we carry out our service.

Now let's say that we feel completely out of our comfort zone because this is not the typical seller. This seller has a child struggling with mental illness, and you can see that the seller is feeling exhausted and in need of encouragement. This may be a time where you quickly say a prayer asking God how you can serve the need that you have identified. You may get a word of encouragement to share with the seller, and you should treat that message like gold and deliver it with care. God gives us what we need at the right time, and we should have confidence in any answer that He provides.

Now let's say that you feel you should offer your help on a regular basis to help the seller pack their belongings because it would take the pressure off them—and you can see that they are overwhelmed. However, you know that this will impact your business because of the time commitment. If we feel called or obliged to engage in something that will be very expensive in time, energy, or resources, we should use discernment before taking action in order to protect ourselves from going in the wrong direction, overextending ourselves, or being taken advantage of. When we understand God's character through the Bible and through prayer, we can discern what is truly a call from God. It may take a little time to engage in conversation with God before making a decision, but it is worth it. If not, you may end up traveling down the wrong path for a long time or encountering unnecessary pain or hardship.

In our personal lives, we should follow the same guidelines for serving others with humility. When we identify needs around us, we should attend to them, stretching ourselves and working outside our comfort zones as we depend on God to help us and asking Him for guidance before taking on bigger commitments. Sometimes God wants us to go big, but we need to ask for His guidance and direction before committing to anything. If God leads us to do something big through His infinite wisdom and ability, we can be sure that we will be successful, no matter how impossible it may seem. If He tells us that we should not engage in something, we can trust that He has other plans for our time and other ways of attending to the need we have identified. God always has a plan, and when we stay in alignment with Him, He works all things for good.

- Do you feel that you serve your clients with humility and care?
- Do you feel that you serve your family and friends with humility and care?
- How do you respond when you feel called to do something that is outside your comfort zone?
    - Is there anything you can do differently to embrace opportunities to serve others when it's not comfortable for you?
    - How do you think that operating in this way would benefit you personally and professionally?
    - Do you lean on God to provide the tools and wisdom that you lack?
- How do you think it makes others feel when you engage in something that is difficult for you?
    - Do you think they feel the difference when you have the green light from God?
    - How do they feel when you haven't checked in with God and you say yes, even though you are stretched thin?
- Are you taking on more than you should by chasing after too many projects?
- How would your life look different if you went to God to help identify your priorities?
    - Would this change the way you feel about the things you engage in?
- When have you asked God to help set your priorities? How did this go?

THE WINDOWS
AND SCREENS

Windows give us vision to the outside world. The way our windows open, and whether they have functional screens, helps us to control what we want to allow into our home. We want windows that are not damaged, that open and close properly, and that can be sealed to the outside weather conditions when needed but opened when we want to let in fresh air. We want screens that are intact so that pests cannot enter our home, while we still can allow the fresh air to flow through.

VISION AND BOUNDARIES

Windows symbolize having vision, using discernment, and setting appropriate boundaries in our personal and professional lives. We need to have eyes to see clearly into the distance and to look at the reality of our options and the things happening around us, as well as the ability to decide when we should open ourselves up to things, and when we should close ourselves off. This is not an easy task and requires wisdom, discernment, and setting boundaries.

For example, you may have an activity in your life that is overall positive but tends to turn bad when you engage in it too often. Maybe you love to swim but when you spend more than thirty minutes at the pool each morning, your day gets offtrack and you end up more stressed than relaxed from that visit to the pool. If you know this, maybe you should only open your window a little, limiting the time you spend at the pool so that you let the right amount of recreation into your day and you are still able to get everything else done in a leisurely way.

Another example could be a person you need to limit your conversations with. Maybe they talk about market data too much, and it takes your focus to a place of fear rather than to serving your customers with excellence. While this person is just trying to be helpful and market data is important to be aware of, you don't want to consume yourself with it because you know that it makes you fearful. In this case, you may need to close your window and only crack it open from time to time so that you can stay on top of what is happening around you.

On the other hand, let's say that you've developed a friendship that is incredibly supportive and loving. Every time you interact with this person, you feel supported, encouraged, and happy. This is where you swing your window wide open. Maybe you even throw off the screen and let them jump right through the window!

Life is all about looking at the opportunities around you, deciding if they are good or bad, and choosing how much you should let in. It takes practice and skill, and it is worth the effort.

- Do you have a good system for evaluating what is happening around you and envisioning what you want to invite into your own life?
    - What works for you?
    - What would you like to start doing to help you with this?
- What boundaries have you set that are helpful to you?
    - How does it affect your work and personal life when you practice keeping good boundaries?

- What boundaries have you set that are too rigid?
  - How does it affect your work and personal life when your boundaries are too rigid?
- Where could you use better boundaries?
  - What are some ways that you can create these boundaries?
- How would your life look if you improved your boundaries?

HELPING OTHERS

Sometimes when helping people we love, we can overextend ourselves because we feel that we should not have boundaries with them. As much as we are built to live in relationship with each other, there is only *one* relationship that we need more than anything, and that is our relationship with God. It's important to remember this because while we may play a part in helping, we should not feel obligated to meet *every* need for someone we love. When someone has a relationship with God, they *don't need* any one person or thing to help them. Help from friends, therapies, material belongings, and other things are helpful—but not satisfying on the level that God is.

How would it feel if you were invited into someone's home for dessert and they gave you a spoonful of frosting, then two, then three, then continued to give you only frosting. This is what it is like when we offer our help to someone in need, trying to satisfy them with our time and attention but not introducing them to God. Not only is this unsatisfying to the person we are helping, but it is exhausting for us as we try to serve them in a way that will never bring satisfaction. God is the actual cake, the substance. And in this case, when friends, family, or clients come to us for help, we should consider ourselves the frosting. This brings proper perspective to the amount of responsibility we actually have and what God expects of us.

When we help people, we should try to help with their practical needs. And in order to bring them true satisfaction, we should share the word of God and the love of God. We can do this in our personal and professional lives by not only fulfilling our role as a family member, friend, or agent but also by speaking truth into people's lives and showing them love. He does not expect us to do the things that only He can do. He only asks that we help in some small ways and turn others to Him so that He can do the *real* work.

The bigger view from our window is that God is the *one* we *all* need. We can slide open a window to help someone when possible, but we don't need to open our windows wide to every person and every situation, thinking that we are responsible for solving every problem. We owe it to ourselves to maintain boundaries and self-control so that we can keep our focus on God, the *one* true God and King of kings, the one who is limitless in wisdom, ability, and love.

This life is temporary, and whether we remember it or not, we are all on a spiritual journey that is far more important than any business transaction, wedding, bank account, family vacation, or anything else we may value in this world. As we work to understand God's wisdom and make ourselves whole, we should offer the same wisdom to others when the opportunity or need arises. If they reject it, we can accept that we did our part and move on. It may seem like we did nothing, but we are fishers of men trying to reel them in. Some may not catch on to what we are offering, but some will. Even if we only catch one in a lifetime, it is worth it and God is pleased. He cares about every individual. He loves His people, and when we are working at returning them to Him, He is pleased, like any loving parent would be over finding a lost child.

- Do you feel that you carry an appropriate amount of re-sponsibility when helping others with their problems?
  - Why? Or why not?
- When have you overextended yourself in helping others?
  - How does it feel when you take on too much responsibility?
  - In what ways is this destructive?
- Where do you need to set better boundaries in your life?
  - How will setting better boundaries in this area affect other areas of your life?
- When have you set appropriate boundaries when helping others?
  - How does it feel when you help others while keeping boundaries?
  - In what ways does this positively affect other areas of your life?
- How does it feel to allow God to do what *only* He can do and let yourself off the hook?

LAUGHTER

One way to screen life's experiences is through humor and laughter. Whenever possible, in all that you experience, note the humor. There is always something funny going on. Laughing lightens our mood and encourages us to carry on. As you laugh, the heaviness of hardship melts away like gentle waves of cotton candy. No one has said that life always has to be taken so seriously, and we can choose happiness no matter what we are facing.

Laughter has real health benefits. It is scientifically proven to decrease stress, relieve depression, release endorphins in your brain, stimulate organs, improve your immune system, relieve inflammation in the body, and do so much more. It also has spiritual benefits.

> A joyful heart is good medicine, but a crushed
> spirit dries up the bones. (Proverbs 17:22)

Incorporate laughter into your day! Find a friend who makes you chuckle, and talk to them *more,* see the irony in situations you face, hang up a funny quote in your office, or listen to your favorite comedian while you drive. There is no wrong way to do it. Just find ways to incorporate more of this into your life, and you will be glad you did.

- When was the last time you really laughed? Who were you with? What were you laughing at?
    - How did it make you feel?
- Who in your life makes you laugh? Who laughs at your jokes or witty comments?
    - Is this someone that you can spend more time with or talk to more often?
- How often do you laugh?
    - Do you need more laughter in your life?
    - What can you do to chuckle more frequently?
- How will more laughter in your life help you in your personal and professional life?

DANGER IN REVIEWS

We need functional screens in place as we anticipate receiving feedback and the wisdom to know when we may need to lock the window and close the curtains. We all love reading a great review from one of our recent clients, praising us for the things we did well and for how we hung the stars for them. We may have hundreds of positive reviews, and we may be feeling extremely confident and encouraged in who we are. But if a negative review finds its way into our feed, it can be like a tiny little needle that bursts our giant bubble of happiness and success. The bubble that was filled with all of our positive thoughts and memories, all of the things we value about ourselves, and all of our self-confidence: deflated. One damaging comment is made, and all of the good is gone and forgotten.

It may seem like the enemy is that one negative comment. However, the enemy is our attachment to what other people think about us and our allowing it to have the power to tear us down. When we hear compliments and praise, it's easy to embrace them and to care deeply about what others are thinking about us. Unfortunately, when that one negative comment creeps in and we are completely attached to what people think about us, that comment is like a dagger shooting straight into our wide-open hearts!

It is best to receive *all* feedback with caution. If we already know who we are to God and are focused on cultivating good for the people we work with, we don't need them to tell us who we are. We know who we are, and this is a steadier and much more secure place to be. When we are settled and secure in who we are and someone says something negative, we can accept the critical feedback and change the way we are doing things if needed, but it will not feel like a personal attack. Because we know who we are, we will be able to consider whether the comments are valid, and we can handle them accordingly. We can evaluate them from an arm's-length distance rather than immediately absorbing them.

At other times, we may receive empty praise from people who are being dishonest—trying to manipulate us or achieve some personal agenda. Or they may be holding back the truth we need to hear for the sake of "being nice." This is why it can be equally important to hold those positive comments out for examination as well, before taking them into our hearts.

An easy way to think about this is to consider what you do with your kid's bag of Halloween candy. You want them to enjoy the goodies, but you don't want them to get hurt. So before they go out trick-or-treating, you make sure that they have first filled up with a nutritious dinner because too much candy will make them sick. Then upon their return from trick-or-treating, you carefully sort through the candy, examining each piece to make sure it is safe and that the wrappers are securely closed. Once the bad pieces have been discarded, you allow them to dig in and enjoy!

In the same way, we need to fill up on an understanding of what God says is true about us and what we know to be true about ourselves. Then we are in the right place to receive some carefully inspected comments, after discarding anything that is harmful or untrue.

- What good can come of reviews?
  - Do customers, friends, or family members consistently praise you for the same qualities or behaviors? What do they praise you for?
  - How does this feedback make you feel?
- How can reviews be damaging?
  - Do customers, friends, or family members regularly criticize you for the same qualities or behaviors? What specifically do they mention?
  - Is the feedback justified? Is there anything you should do differently?
  - Is any of the feedback not justified? Do you need to release it?
  - How do these critical reviews make you feel?
- Do critical comments from others regarding your performance upset you? Why?
- Do you depend on what others say about you to determine your value?

- Do you take all feedback to heart, or do you examine it carefully?
    - How would your life be different if you put less importance on what others say about you?
- What honest feedback would you give yourself in each area of your life?
    - What do you need to work on?
    - What are you doing well?

COSMETIC FINISHES

The aesthetic condition of walls, paint, light fixtures, and flooring may not impact the way your home functions, but these finishes do enhance the way we live. If the finishes are in good condition, you enjoy your home and it is inviting for guests. The condition of the finishes also has an impact on the appraised value of your house. If the finishes are in subpar condition, you may feel uncomfortable in your home and it may not feel as welcoming to others. It will also contribute to how much you make when selling the house. This is the superficial part of your house, but it still contributes to the overall integrity of the house in a very big way. In the same way, our bodies and the way we dress and carry ourselves may be superficial to some degree, but they are extremely important in the way we live, how others engage with us, and maybe even how much we earn.

HEALTHY LIFESTYLE

If you've been watching too much reality TV, you may compare yourself to celebrity real estate agents selling luxury homes. Their expensive clothing gives them the polish they need to win every listing, and as they drive away in their Lamborghinis and Bentleys, the signed listing in hand, other agents are envious.

In the evenings they may drink champagne in a mansion or on a yacht. They are fit, their skin is flawless, and their friends are many.

Some may compare themselves to cultural idols cherishing the superficial and artificial things in life. Focusing on these things will inevitably lead to disappointment. It's kind of like cherishing a plastic cake that was created for staging a house. It looks perfect but has no flavor, and it is not something that anyone would actually want to eat. A homemade cake, on the other hand, may be beautiful but will have some imperfections. It will not *look* perfect, but it will taste incredible, and you will feel the love when you are eating it.

Of course, there is nothing wrong with having an expensive car, a great physique, and flawless skin. My point is that we should not place more importance on superficial things than we do on things of substance. No honest agent would advise a client to buy a home with new paint, gorgeous landscaping, and stunning staging while knowing that the paint is hiding mold and the rugs are covering stains on the flooring. In the same way, we want to focus on our bodies for the right reasons! We want it to function properly so that it supports us in our activities. Imagine engaging in extreme dieting. You may look great, but your mind doesn't function properly because it is not being nourished properly. This would be an example of focusing on your body in the wrong ways. On the other hand, if we eat nourishing meals, our bodies may or may not look the way we want it to, but we have the energy we need to take care of the people around us. And chances are that we look great too. And beyond this, maybe we don't always make perfect choices for our physical health and indulge in some ice cream, but we enjoy it with someone we love. This can also be very important, and we should be flexible so that we don't miss out on something wonderful.

Of course, there are many elements to consider when caring

for our bodies. Part of this is how we eat, but it also includes good sleep habits and exercise. A good night's sleep improves brain function, mood, and overall health. Exercise promotes endorphins, creative thinking, and stress relief and promotes health. When your body is healthy, you can complete the tasks you need to at an optimal level, and your mind is free when undistracted by ailments and stress.

- What habits are you engaging in that promote good health?
    - How do these habits benefit you personally and professionally?
- What does your body need right now?
    - How can you integrate some new, healthy habits into your daily routine?
- How will it feel when you are taking better care of your body?
- How does a healthy lifestyle affect your life personally and professionally?

APPEARANCE

The way we dress and the way we carry ourselves are also important. We can't get around the fact that we are first evaluated by the way we look. Although this can become a superficial obsession, we can steer clear of this by evaluating on a deeper level. The way we dress should reflect who we are, what is important to us, and how others should see us. The way we carry ourselves includes our posture, our facial expressions, our hairstyle, our clothing, etc.

For example, you may on the surface see that someone has a clean, neat appearance. Their hair is styled fashionably and their clothes fit them well and have been pressed. They are standing tall with confidence, and on their face, we see a comforting smile of love and appreciation. They've attended to every detail, their physical appearance is pleasing to the eye, and they carry themselves with confidence. Because of the way they look, you may conclude that this person is kind and confident and cares about themselves and the people around them. You may conclude that they are trustworthy and detailed in their work.

On the other hand, if you saw someone with a disheveled and unclean appearance, slouching and wearing a frown, you may assume that they do not care about themselves or others, that they are lazy or unintelligent, and they may not inspire your trust. We want to send a clear message to those around us that we are someone they should engage with, personally and professionally. This is something that we have control over, by making the choice to present ourselves in a positive light.

- How do you dress? Think carefully about how you show up.
  - What would you think if you saw another person show up in the way you do at home, in social settings, or at work?
  - What does your physical appearance say to the people around you?
- In what ways can you improve your appearance?
- Are there any practical habits you can incorporate into your daily grooming and dressing routine that would improve your look?
- How will attending to your appearance change your life?

PEOPLE ARE PEOPLE

As we care for our own bodies, *it's important to remember that our clients are also human. They have the same needs that we do!* Consider all of the psychological and physiological needs of a human being. Maslow's hierarchy of needs may or may not be a complete list of needs but gives some great insights. It highlights self-actualization (which is achieving our full potential), esteem (which is feeling accomplished and respected), belonging and love (which includes relationships of all kinds), and security and safety. It also notes physiological needs, such as food, water, warmth, and rest.

While working to be the best at our roles in our professional and personal lives, we should not forget that we are engaging with human beings. Humans are instinctively hungry, tired, need hugs and encouragement, and are moved when they see a smile. We all have the same basic needs.

When serving a client, we are missing a huge opportunity for connection if we forget to smile, share a kind word, offer security by advocating for them, help them avoid burnout during their home search by streamlining the process, or fail to bring them bottles of cold water when touring homes on a hot day.

If we learn all of the most powerful sales and contract skills or understand the intricacies of real estate investment but overlook basic needs, the service we extend will fall flat. If we want a true impact on people's lives, we must make sure that basic needs are met as we provide all of the other aspects of our service because this brings about a deeper connection. Providing substance that incorporates a person's basic needs may be something that clients are unable to put their finger on, but they will be drawn to you and the services you provide because they feel satisfied on a deeper level. Connection is what gives us purpose and ties people to each other in both business and personal relationships. It promotes satisfaction in giving and in receiving.

- How do you attend to the basic needs of people in your life?
    - How do you do this with friends and family?

      o   How do you do this with clients and colleagues?
      o   What difference does it make in their lives and in your own life?
- What specific things can you do to improve the way you serve others?
      o   What difference will it make?

When considering that every person has the same basic needs, let's also think about how this applies to our real estate clients who are buying or selling at different price points. Deciding that a client who appears to be highly successful or experienced should be treated differently from your typical client or feeling overwhelmed or intimidated by the price tag on a house is common for many agents. However, these differences are illusions.

The truth is that every person has the same basic needs, and your value as an agent, and as a human being, does not change based on who you offer your services to. While you may tailor your communication to a particular person a little differently in order to relate to them or meet them where they are, you will still communicate the same things when guiding them through the transaction. And if it is effective for one person, it will be for another.

It is also true that every real estate transaction carries the same fundamental principles, activities, and processes. This does not change depending on price. When we believe a higher-priced home will be more challenging to sell or purchase, we are being driven by fear rather than by reality.

The reality is that people are people and houses are houses.

- Do you feel that you are capable of bringing value to every potential client, regardless of price point, education level, or any other factor?
      o   Why? Or why not?

- Which clients make you feel the least comfortable?
    - How does it feel when you are unsure about serving this type of client?
    - What has led you to believe that they need to be treated differently?
- Which clients make you most comfortable?
    - How do you feel and behave when working with these clients?
    - How do these feelings and behaviors lead to success?
    - What are you doing with this group of people that you are not doing with others?
    - Why are you serving them differently?
- What specific things can you do for every client that will lead to success?
    - How will it feel when you are comfortable serving every type of person?
    - How will this affect your level of success?

ENVIRONMENTAL

ELIMINATE PESTS

A pest is an annoyance and a nuisance in a house and can be very destructive. Think about the damage tiny termites can do as they eat through walls and tear down an entire house in a matter of years. Or consider the disgust you would feel if mice or roaches were crawling on your floors. In life, a pest can be something that we struggle with—like addiction, anger, resentment, unforgiveness, an emotional issue, or engaging in gossip.

Let's talk about gossip. On the surface, it may seem pretty harmless—fun—and we may even invite this into our lives. Gossip usually makes us feel connected with the people we are dishing it with as we unite in our hatred or judgment of someone else outside the conversation. However, this pest is poisonous and destructive to us, to the others engaging in it with us, and to the person who the gossip is about. When someone gossips with you about someone else, chances are that they will gossip about you. This means that you cannot trust them. They also can't trust you! What appears to be connection is actually extreme disconnection. The other issue is that you really don't know what is going on in the life of the person you are gossiping about. Once you find out, you may feel horrible for making their difficult situation worse by sharing things that were private for them—or maybe even sharing things that were not fully true. Sharing things that are true, praise-worthy, and kind are always better conversation topics and do not backfire on you or others. Beyond this, if there is something bothering us about someone, we should develop the courage and the tools we need to talk directly to them, building up the relationship rather than talking about them to someone else and making things complicated for ourselves and others.

Another sneaky pest is blame. Blame is a very common tendency, seems relatively harmless, and can create *big* roadblocks to our success. Blame feels good in the moment but can be very destructive in relationships and in outcomes. Real estate transactions are all about relationships with our clients, the other agent, our title company, inspectors, and lenders. It can be a stressful business because there are many challenges faced in every transaction. If we blame others, whether or not it is their fault, we end up angry, which is scientifically proven to make us less intelligent and lessens our ability to find solutions. It is a big distraction from getting things done and making progress. Taking ownership and responsibility for *what you can do* to make each situation better is a much better approach. Sometimes this takes extra time and work on your part, as well as some grace, empathy, and forgiveness, but it is worth it.

An example of a very destructive pest is addiction. This may start as a small pest and grow into a monster. Addiction comes in many forms. But whatever the addiction is, it is clouding your awareness and stealing your focus, time, energy, and ultimately your life. Some addictions can be overcome simply by making a decision and working toward a solution. Others may need medical or professional intervention. And we must remember that anything we take to God, in an effort to become more of the person He made us to be, will be welcomed by Him. He may bring conviction to your heart about a change that needs to be made, but He does not deliver shame. He is a loving Father, and He knows that you are in a spiritual battle while living your life on earth. He wants to help you. So if you are struggling with any kind of addiction, please go to your Father. He will show you what to do and will hold your hand all the way through it to the other side.

Like a termite, any pest that affects you may seem small, but over time, its effects are extreme. We carry our pests into everything we care about in life, and they only bring destruction. The pests have to go! You owe it to yourself and to the people around you. However, it is not easy to overcome pests like this, and it takes practice to master. Be patient with yourself as you work on eliminating pests. Be patient with others as everyone is doing the best they know how to do and no one is perfect. Here is a beautiful prayer that illustrates what your mindset could look like, when free of pests:

> Lord, make me an instrument of your peace; where there is hatred, let me sow love; where there is injury, pardon; where there is doubt, faith; where there is despair, hope; where there is darkness, light; and where there is sadness, joy. O Divine Master, grant that I may not so much seek to be consoled as to console; to be understood, as to understand; to be loved, as to love; for it is in giving that we receive, it is in pardoning that we are pardoned, and it is in dying that we are born to Eternal Life. Amen. (St. Francis of Assisi)

- Identify any pests that are present for you. How does each pest affect each area of your life?
- Why do you engage in the behavior(s)?
  o Do any of the pests come from the same root issue?
- How can you exterminate them?

- Think about how refreshing it will be when your house is free of pests. How would it feel to be free of them in your life?
- How will your life look and feel different from how it is today?

THE PEOPLE AROUND YOU

Evaluating the neighbors may not be part of a traditional home inspection, but they definitely impact how you enjoy your home. Think about the different experiences you've had with neighbors. Some neighbors can be amazing and make you feel comfortable when you drive down the street to your house as they wave from their garden. They are people you can trust to look out for your best interests, whether it is watching your house when you are gone or letting you borrow a couple of eggs when you are short. They take care of their yards and uphold the value of the neighborhood. Bad neighbors, on the other hand, make you cringe when you see them outside. You know that they are bringing destruction to the neighborhood and that they cannot be trusted.

In the same way, the people we surround ourselves with at home and at work are extremely important to our wellbeing and can affect every area of our lives. We should regularly evaluate our relationships and determine if they are healthy and conducive to the things we want in our lives or if they are damaging us in some way.

The people who encourage us, love us, and are willing to work through difficult situations are the people we want in our lives. We need to make the effort to show them they are valued and spend time with them. This includes *every* person we value, whether family, friends, clients, vendors we engage with, or anyone else. Again, we are one person who cannot be divided, and we carry every experience we have into every part of our lives. The more quality relationships that we have, the more every relationship in our lives will be elevated.

For example, if we have particular clients who appreciate us and introduce us to others needing to buy and sell, these are great relationships to have. As we continue to build these relationships and pour out our appreciation, we can expect that they will reciprocate by introducing us to even more of their family and friends who want to buy or sell a home. Your spouse, kids, and friends will benefit from the positivity as well because the people we experience affect our moods, mindset, and the things we talk about. In this example, it even affects our earnings and how we take care of ourselves and our families financially.

On the other hand, if you have people in your life who don't believe in you, continually put you down, and are unwilling to change their behavior, you may want to walk away. This includes personal and professional relationships of all kinds. For example, if we have a toxic customer who is unkind and unappreciative, we should move away from them as quickly as possible because they will hamper our production and bring us down. Every other relationship in our life will also be strained as long as we are connected to someone who is toxic.

Jesus told His disciples to shake the dust from their feet when they are not embraced in a town. This meant that they should shake it off and move on, letting go of rejection, and finding those who will embrace their message. I like to think of this dust as not only rejection but as any quality in a relationship that is destructive. If you have spoken with someone honestly about what you need from them to make the relationship healthy and they are unwilling to change their behavior, it may be time to move on. Sometimes shaking the dust from your feet is a quick and simple action. However, when these relationships are more complicated and long-standing, they can leave a residue that is more like mud than dirt, and it's not always easy to shake it off.

Sometimes it is simple to alter a relationship with some candid conversation or boundary setting. Other times it is difficult and painful as you may need to eliminate someone from your daily interactions. Dealing with negative relationships head-on lightens your load and any messiness as you travel forward in life. When you are not carrying the negativity from these relationships in your life, you have the freedom to walk steadily into new relationships without contaminating them. It's always worth it to clean up your relationships.

Think about the people you interact with every day, including family, friends, colleagues, clients, and acquaintances.

- Who brings out the best in you? How specifically?
- What relationships are unhealthy? How specifically?
- How does each relationship make you feel?
- How does each relationship affect other areas of your life and other people in your life?
- What can you do to maintain healthier relationships?
- How will having healthy relationships change the way you live?

YOUR CRITICS

Critics can be customers, competing agents, associates, family, friends, social media followers, and sometimes ourselves.

Any time we choose to do something new, there is a learning curve. Most people do not wake up and find themselves to be an expert or an instant success in something and have to work at it. Even though we know this, it can be unnerving to put yourself out there with the chance of failing and facing criticism. But if you don't do it, regrets or resentments can build up. In order to enjoy life and find success, we have to walk out the door, allow the sun to hit our faces, and allow people to say what they will.

I recently heard someone say, "You can be great, or you can be safe, but you cannot be both." I believe that with God we are always safe, no matter how we may feel. If we are looking for security in money or fame, we may be disappointed. If we are looking for whatever God wants to achieve, it may come with money or fame, but it may not. It may come with building your character or encouraging someone else who needs it, in order to achieve some other purpose God has. If we are in alignment with God, we are looking for God's outcomes, not what the world tells us we should achieve. God is much bigger than we are, and we need to remember that He has a plan and purpose for each of His children. Following His guidance will lead us to greatness, maybe some discomfort, and definitely safety as we anchor ourselves to Him.

This being said, we still have to deal with critics who will surface in our lives. If we don't have a plan, we will likely crumble under the weight of their judgment. It takes strength and resilience to carry on with your plans in the midst of criticism. We get this strength from knowing who God says we are and also from the people in our lives who encourage us. God continually reminds us in scripture that man has no real power over us. "What can man do to us?" We need to remember that the threat of another person's judgment is empty.

We also need to make sure that we are intentional about focusing on the people who love us rather than on those who discourage or dismiss us. It can be frustrating when people don't accept and embrace us, so we may feel compelled to direct our focus on them, trying to win their love and respect. Instead we need to have the self-discipline to accept that there will always be people who choose to create resistance for us. We can strengthen ourselves to plow through criticism by learning to change our focus to those who accept us and to fill up on their encouragement.

What we need to recognize is that we are doing something in the world that makes a difference, using our unique gifts and purpose. There are no two people who are made equally, and there is no point in comparing ourselves to others or to the standards of our culture. We need to hold our heads high as we walk through the arrows that are flying past us, knowing that they cannot hurt us if we choose to continue moving forward.

> It is not the critic who counts; not the man who points out how the strong man stumbles, or where the doer of deeds could have done them better. The credit belongs to the man who is actually in the arena, whose face is marred by dust and sweat and blood; who strives valiantly; who errs, who comes short again and again, because there is no effort without error and shortcoming; but who does actually strive to do the deeds; who knows great enthusiasms, the great devotions; who spends himself in a worthy cause; who at the best knows in the end the triumph of high achievement, and who at the worst, if he fails, at least fails while daring greatly, so that his place shall never be with those cold and timid souls who neither know victory nor defeat. (Theodore Roosevelt)

- When have you experienced criticism for putting yourself or your work out there?
  - How did this feel?
- How do you typically respond to criticism?
- Who encourages you and makes you feel safe to express yourself?
  - How do you show up differently in life when you are supported?

- Who do you usually focus your attention on: critics or supporters?
- How can you shift your focus more to those who support and encourage you?
- How would this change your life?

RELATIONSHIPS

Relationships are amazing when we are intentional about them and when we understand how God intended for us to operate in them. Relationships can be terrible when we have a poor understanding of their purpose, our roles in them, and when we do not set proper boundaries.

There are so many cultural messages that seep into our consciousness about what it means to have a great friendship or what family should look like. If you think about it, even from childhood we get ideas from fairy tales and movies about what it will be like in romantic relationships, in friendships, and in family.

But the truth is that there are no actual rules about what is "normal." For example, when we hear clichés like "Family is everything," it can be very misleading. Some people don't have a family, and believing that could cause some issues if they believe that their life does not look the way it's "supposed" to look. In reality this person may have a lot of good in their life, even without family. Maybe they have amazing friends or more time to spend using their talents to serve the world.

What if another person hearing the same message, "Family is everything," was being abused by family members? Would they continue to allow abuse, believing that family should be valued above all else? You can see how these types of generalized cultural beliefs can create damage and dysfunction in a person's life.

The same kinds of general cultural messages can impact how

we feel about our friendships. We may hear that "true friends last a lifetime." But in reality, some friends are with us for a season. Even though it may not fit the mold that our culture has given us, we can appreciate the friendship and recognize its value. There are many different types of friends, and each stays in our lives for various amounts of time. When we drop the rules and measurements we've been given by our society or culture, we are free to see things as they truly are.

Beyond all of this, the Bible tells us that God is everything; God comes first. There is a reason that He should be our first priority—and everything falls into its proper place when He is. God gives us very clear guidelines in the Bible about relationships, what they should look like, and how we should handle the personal and business situations we encounter. God is the only one who is all-knowing, who is perfectly loving, who never leaves your side, and who is faithful always, from the time He created you in your mother's womb until the time you join Him in eternal life. When we follow His instructions, we find security in our support structure and our interactions. If we believe every cultural message that we hear, we can really get offtrack in our minds and hearts. We need to be careful about what we accept as the truth.

If you are thinking that this seems like a lot to consider, you are right! It takes time to unpack all of the false beliefs we've accumulated about relationships and to embrace the truth. Once this is done, it takes effort to develop positive, fulfilling relationships. The good news is that you can work at it step by step, day by day. No one on this planet is perfect, and no one should expect you to be perfect (including you).

Everyone is different, and it's important to honor this by being honest with yourself and others about what you need and want. The clearer you are about this in your own mind, and the more you voice these things out loud, the more likely you are to end up with the right people in your life. And because relationships are a two-way street, you need to consider what the people in your life need from you. We should do our best to show up whole-heartedly for the people in our lives. We owe it to them, and we owe it to ourselves.

- What false beliefs have you accepted about relationships?
- How have these beliefs affected the way you approach relationships?
    o Has this been helpful or harmful? In what ways?
- What is the reality that you need to face in your relationships?
    o How will facing reality affect you and the people around you?
    o What would the benefit be to choosing reality over cultural clichés?
- What can you do to learn more about what God teaches us to be true about relationships?

MAKE IT SPARKLE

Now that all of the house has been inspected and repaired, and we've evaluated the neighborhood, we can focus on cleaning the superficial part of the house that everyone sees when they walk through it. We get the kitchens and bathrooms sparkling like new, the floors perfectly polished and gleaming, and the windows free of dust and streaks. We mow the lawn and paint the fence. Then we make our favorite beverage and enjoy the view from our patio. We have a new lease on life! When your house sparkles, it is the clearest and most obvious communication to those who experience it that it is clean and operating effectively. You are not tripping over boxes or distracted by a mess. It is not complicated or flawed. All you see is a concise statement of function and beauty.

When we sparkle as people, we are no longer burdened by the things that have been weighing us down and causing us dysfunction. We are not only showing the world a positive view of who we are, but we are also in good repair and clean from the inside out! This is where we can truly shine and show the world what we are capable of and who we were made to be. Our life's purpose can be fulfilled much more easily because we are standing on a solid rock, a foundation that is unmoving and filled with purpose. The storms going on around us cannot affect us because we are solid and secure. We are a force to be reckoned with in our personal and our professional lives. Because we are functional and have clarity, we are much clearer and more effective in communicating our vision and intentions to others. We "sparkle" with clarity.

MASTER YOUR WORDS

In order to sparkle with clarity, we need to be intentional with our communication. Just like when we make our houses sparkle, good communication requires a decision—and some elbow grease.

When you are intentional with your words, you make every word count, and you can be more productive. Good communication is one of our biggest superpowers as people and as agents. If you think about positive experiences you've had with other people, either personally or in business, you can attribute much of the great experience to the way they communicated with you. We need to be focused and intentional when choosing our words.

Our tongues are like rudders on boats, and just as we need to make sure that the rudder is pointed in the right direction, we need to make sure that our words are aligned to take us to the right place. Maybe we want someone to know how much we care or we want them to take a specific action to help them achieve their goal. There are a few simple ways to make sure that this happens.

1. Honesty is always the best way to keep things moving in the right direction. Even a white lie with the best of intentions can take us offtrack.
2. Simplicity! There is no need to use fancy vocabulary or professional jargon. We want our message to be understood and well-received, so we need to make it easy.
3. A concise message is easy to digest. When a message is not filled with clutter, people can easily see the point you are trying to make and will be more receptive.

4. Keep the message positive. Negativity is a turnoff and creates fear and uncertainty. Any message, even when navigating a difficult situation, can be presented in a positive light by tying it to the ultimate goal someone is trying to achieve or by tying it to the fact that you care and want things to go well for the other person.

5. Be intentional! While elaborate and deep conversation can be pleasant, we need to be aware of times when it is not helpful. When trying to get something done in a transaction or personal situation, sometimes the best thing we can do for the other person is to take a very intentional and direct approach, focused on what needs to be addressed. Sometimes it helps to write out your thoughts before making a phone call to make sure you've identified what is important, providing yourself with a guide for the conversation.

The more you can learn about verbal and nonverbal communication, the better you will perform. You can read books, attend classes, and watch instructional videos. You can also observe the responses you get to certain things you say. If the result you get is not what you anticipated, try something new.

- Think about a time when someone said something to you that was very impactful.
  - How did their words make you feel?
  - Did they motivate you to take action on something? Why? Or why not?
- Answer the following questions, and then consider how each is hurting or helping you in your work and personal relationships:
  - How honest are you in your communication?
  - How simple is your communication?

- o   Is your communication clear and concise?
- o   Do you consider whether your communication will come across in a positive way?
- o   Are you intentional about what is important to say in each conversation and how brief or elaborate your conversation should be?

MAKE SURE THEY KNOW

Sometimes we think about things so much that we think we have communicated them to the people around us. In reality, the people around us have no idea what we are thinking and we are fooling ourselves by believing that they know. It is important that we communicate *out loud,* and that we do this honestly.

When it comes to our clients, it is important that we are truly leading them through the process of buying and selling. We want to be proactive, setting the stage for success, rather than reactive and cleaning up messes. This takes strong and intentional communication. We need to set appropriate boundaries and expectations and guide them through each step in the transaction. Sometimes we are afraid that our direct communication will come off as pushy or that they will misunderstand our intentions. However, if the essence of what we want to communicate is related to their needs and to helping them find success, we *need* to communicate it. It's all about *why* we are saying it, and *how* we say it.

Sharing our strategies and why we are taking a particular action is important. It may seem fussy to explain strategy, but if we don't, it may diminish trust and make the process more difficult for everyone. If we clearly explain our thought process and why we are suggesting a particular path for them, they can easily come into alignment with us because they understand the reasons behind what we are doing and we have explained it in a way that they can digest. This will keep everyone on the same page while earning respect and trust from the client.

Throughout our communication, we also need to articulate that we are in the client's corner and serving their best interests, making sure they understand how that ties to the things we are explaining, regarding our thought process and strategy. We may think our customers already know, assuming that they clearly see that we are trying to set things up in their favor. However, if we don't come out and clearly state this, they may not know. They may come to their own conclusions about why we are doing or saying things in the way that we are, and they may draw the wrong conclusions. If we actually tell them out loud, we can be sure that they come to the right conclusions about our intentions for them.

- Are you comfortable being direct in your communication with people?
  - When and why do you do this?
  - Do you feel it is helpful or harmful to the relationship? In what ways?
- Are there times when you hold back from being direct?
  - When and why do you do this?
  - Do you feel it is helpful or harmful to the relationship? In what ways?

KEEP IT SIMPLE

When our houses are functional and clean, there is nothing complicated about this. We love to be in a clean environment where everything is simple and beautiful. In the same way, I believe it is the agent's job to make the process of buying or selling a house simple and enjoyable. However, making it simple requires a lot of work in the background as you refine the way you guide someone through the process. It takes time and effort to develop this skill.

Beyond coming up with a great process, simplicity requires humility because simplicity does not involve showing off everything we know or putting ourselves in the spotlight. It is moving ourselves to the side and selflessly using what we know to create an easy path for someone to get what they want. When this skill is really strong, a client may think the process was so easy that they did not need your involvement. You definitely want your client to know that you are the reason the experience is smooth, and this is also a skill that needs to be developed. You can give your client an awareness of the ways you are creating a smooth path for them without distracting from the great experience. This is a delicate balance that brings great rewards for everyone involved.

- What kind of experience do you create for your clients?
  - What are you doing well?
  - What could be better?
- Do you feel that you make the transaction process simple or complicated?
  - In what ways?
  - Are there certain areas that you should improve? What will you do differently?
- Do you consistently let others know what you are doing to help them?
  - When and why do you do this in your personal life and at work?
  - Do you feel it is helpful or harmful to the relationship? In what ways?
  - Are there ways that you could improve the way you communicate this?

DECORATION

Once you've done your inspections, made some needed repairs, checked out the neighborhood, and cleaned, you can move on to the fun part! Decorate your life and your profession with all of the things that make it successful and enjoyable. Of course, you will still do regular inspections and maintenance from time to time, to maintain the integrity of your home, but you now have a good foundation and base to build on, so have some fun! Adjust your existing decor, or completely revamp it.

When you think of decorating your home, this includes lighting, space, line, form, color, and texture. You want it to be functional, visually appealing, and comfortable for the activities you are engaging in. With this idea in mind, think about your professional decor as the things that really differentiate you from the competition and that show off your best qualities: your new thought patterns, habits, and the repertoire of skills you use when working with clients and selling houses. Think about how the new things you have developed internally translate to your business externally. Maybe you need to revamp your web site, take some updated branding photos, or even redesign your logo. You may want to change the way you dress or rewrite your mission statement.

Of course every area of your life is important, and you should give the same amount of time and energy to each area, including your faith, marriage, kids, friends, family, clients, finances, recreation, dreams, etc. Think deeply about how you want to decorate your life. Journaling can be helpful to flesh out your thoughts completely. Consider the big-picture vision you have for your life.

- How do you want your personal and professional life to look and feel?
- What purpose do you feel God gave you in each area of your life?
- What will success look like for you?
- What actions do you need to take in order to make your life look and feel this way?

CURATE YOUR LIFE

When decor is not focused and intentional, we might say the space looks "busy." This is what happens when we have too much going on in a room. We may have too much furniture, too many colors or patterns, or too many accessories. While everything in the space may be beautiful on its own, when everything is in the room together, it is too much.

On the other hand, our decor may feel sterile and lifeless because we have not taken the risk to purchase items for our home and put them together in a pleasing way. We may be holding ourselves back from the beauty that is possible for us.

In order to make the space flow, avoid the "busyness," and infuse life into a sterile space, we need to curate the space with the items that really give it that *wow* factor. We need to start with the layout and the bigger furniture items, choosing what fits the scale of the space and what brings function and comfort to it. Then we may start filling the space with larger items, like rugs and accent tables. Finally, we will choose smaller accessories to represent the design, like art, plants, and pillows. We may have to get rid of the abundance of furnishings and decor items we had before, but now the space lives up to what it can be. This makes it easy to part with those things that previously cluttered the space. Or if we did not have enough to fill the space, we may have needed to take a leap of faith and bring those beautiful and meaningful items into our homes.

In our lives, we can also accumulate too much "busyness." Busyness is usually associated with multitasking and juggling many priorities. When someone asks how we are doing, most of us proudly state how busy we are because this is usually valued in our society. While it may feel like we are accomplishing a lot and displaying the wonderful quality of being a hard worker, we feel rushed and frantic. We may end up only doing reactive, shallow work and be left with many unfinished projects or having to do tasks over again after not doing them correctly or completely the first time.

On the other hand, we may be keeping our lives sterile because we don't want to make a choice on what to pursue. In reality, we must make the choice to do something because that's what gives life purpose and excitement. We can never really dive into meaningful pursuits and see the fruits of our labor if we are biting off too little. And the beauty of taking a huge bite into the things you want to do is that nothing is final. You are a creative being, and with a change in desires or plans, you can make a new choice and change your path at any time.

When we are rushing through life or are fragmented in our attention, we miss so much of the beauty, abundance, and opportunity that are here for us. Contrary to what we may believe, we typically get the best results when we work deliberately and intentionally, focused on the things that matter the most. When we focus on the things that matter, we can be productive rather than busy. When we slow down, we can work with purpose, sticking to a single task and engaging in deep work. This is a more relaxed and enjoyable way to work and brings about quality and satisfaction. It can be difficult to work in this way with so many things competing for our attention. This is why we must identify our priorities in life each day, and within each hour, and choose where to spend our time and energy. It can take time and effort to figure out how to balance everything and develop effective time-management skills, but the payoff is great.

Being in the present moment is powerful. When we are fully present, we are not worried about the future or regretful about the past. This is where we truly experience life, find solutions to problems, and make the people around us feel seen and heard. This is the place where we find gratitude and happiness.

When working with clients, spending time with friends and family or our pets, or enjoying time alone, tapping into the power of the present moment and thus giving each person, activity, and moment your full awareness and attention, it is life-changing. This is where you find the essence of who you truly are and of who God is. God is always present in every moment, and when we slow down, we experience His love, tap into His wisdom, and draw from His strength. Use the power you have, and experience the comfort and joy in your life. It's here for you right now!

- Are you taking on a manageable number of projects, biting off more than you can chew, or not engaging in enough?
    - o How does this affect your business and your personal life?
    - o Is there anything you would like to change? In what ways?

GRATITUDE

When we have a beautifully decorated home, it can affect us emotionally. Think about a design show you've seen where the designer turns the new and improved house over to the home-owners. They may have looks of complete awe and shock at how beautiful their homes are. They may scream in excitement or cry because they are so grateful. However, *maintaining* gratitude takes work and intention, just like everything else that is good in our lives. Because we get accustomed to all of the good in our lives, it's easy to forget how wonderful things are unless we create the habit of keeping gratitude at the forefront of our minds. It's been said that when we are feeling grateful for what we have, we have everything. Gratitude can change what we see and how we experience the world.

In the movie theater, we may put on plastic glasses to trans-port us from a flat 2D encounter to an exciting 3D experience. When we have 3D vision, everything comes alive, our perspective has a greater sense of depth, and we feel more connected to every-thing happening on the screen, because it feels like it is happening to us and all around us.

When we walk through our actual life in 2D, we feel flat and unaffected. We feel like an observer and may be entertained but not deeply affected or moved. When we walk through life charged with gratitude, we enter the 3D experience. In the reality of life, it's not as easy as throwing on a pair of magic glasses, and it takes practice to experience this shift of perspective. However, once we achieve this, and as we build an "attitude of gratitude," the experience is similar. We are transported into a place where we come alive. Because the good around us is magnified, it affects us deeply. We do not feel like observers; we are participants engaged in the beauty and wonder of life.

Finding ways to practice gratitude is important, and you can easily find one or more techniques to work into your daily routine. Maybe it is thinking of all that you are thankful for as you engage in your morning run. Maybe you write down three things that you are grateful for each day, practice mindfulness in your daily activities, noting all of the good around you, celebrate small wins, or thank the people around you. There are so many things you can do beyond what is listed here. Find some ways to practice and ignite your happiness! If you really want to see your world erupt in bliss, get your family or your coworkers involved in practicing gratitude with you. This will magnify both your experience and theirs.

- Are you seeing the world through a lens of gratitude? Why? Or why not?
- How can you improve your gratitude practice?
   o How will this change your life?
- What are you most thankful for in your life right now?

HANGING STRING LIGHTS

The thought of hanging string lights makes most people think of a special event or occasion and is often associated with festive, sentimental, or loving feelings. We use string lights on our Christmas trees and for our New Year celebrations. We use them at weddings and other important celebrations, or even when we just want to feel cozy. They simply make us feel good!

So when you feel the urge to celebrate your success, hang up some string lights and enjoy the glow. You may not literally hang string lights—or maybe you do! Either way, hanging string lights represents physically doing something to acknowledge how far you've come and all of the wonderful things that are happening in your life. This is not something that you have to postpone until everything is perfect. The key here is to stop and enjoy all that you are building in life.

The thing to consider about real or figurative string lights is that they don't just magically appear. Just like all of the work we've done to become the purest and best version of ourselves, no one can do it for us. It's up to us to choose to do the work and to make life a better place for ourselves and the people around us. We have to hang them intentionally, creating the mood so that we can invite others to help celebrate the event.

Life will never be perfect, and we as individuals will never be perfect until we reunite with our Creator. But for now, we can enjoy our progress and achievements, knowing that we've put in the work to bring about purity in our lives to the greatest degree possible. We've made the repairs, cleaned the house, decorated, and can now truly connect with the people in our lives in a more impactful and meaningful way.

Because we have seized opportunities for improvement, maximized what we have to offer, and are acting from a place of purpose, we will want to be surrounded by the same kinds of people—people who are being intentional in the way they shape their lives. When we have solid relationships built on a strong foundation, love, and healthy boundaries, we can truly have purity, connection, and joy in our lives. And when we all gather together, it can resemble what God taught us about loving Him and loving others as we love ourselves. This is *true* purity and connection and what every human being longs for.

Imagine a long wooden table on the grass, surrounded by trees, the sound of music and laughter filling the air, the smell of pinon and cedar burning in the outdoor fireplace, and flickering candles on the table, where everyone is enjoying the finest foods and drinks, bonding, and laughing warmly under the string lights *you* hung.

The light of all of the hard work you have done in your own life will make the people living under your light feel valued, warm, and loved. And beyond this, the lights you hung, representing all of the wisdom you have gained and the changes you have made in your life, will be an invitation to others to do the same, encouraging them that it is possible. My hope for you is that the lights on your string light will be plentiful and that your joy will be immense.

You are a masterpiece and were created with a purpose. I wish you success and fullness of joy in your life and in your business, so abundantly that it overflows to those around you. May you be someone who brings glory to God and brings others hope and joy.

Thank you for reading *Finding Your Joy!*

Who do you know that would benefit from reading this book? Joy is abundant and there's more than enough to go around. Spread the joy by sharing the title of this book with others.

On the following pages, jot down your thoughts about anything that you want to remember as you continue your journey.

Visit RockRealEstateCoaching.com

Sound Wisdom with Real Results

Resources available for real estate agents,
home buyers, and home sellers.

Things to Consider More Deeply

Specific Action Steps I Will Take to Improve Myself

Specific Action Steps I Will Take to Help Others

Key Takeaways

Visit RockRealEstateCoaching.com

Sound Wisdom with Real Results

Resources available for real estate agents,
home buyers, and home sellers.

Printed in the USA
CPSIA information can be obtained
at www.ICGtesting.com
LVHW040844210824
788836LV00002B/335